# Hello! 150 Wine Recipes

## (Wine Recipes - Volume 1)

## Best Wine Cookbook Ever For Beginners

Ms. Ingredient

# Content

# Introduction

***

Why I Love Cooking

Hi all,

Welcome to MrandMsCooking.com—a website created by a community of cooking enthusiasts with the goal of providing books for novice cooks featuring the best recipes, at the most affordable prices, and valuable gifts.

Before we go to the recipes in the book "Hello! 150 Wine Recipes", I have an interesting story to share with you the reason for loving cooking.

My mom would always tell me:

Cooking is an edible form of love…

As a young kid, I helped my mom cook. She would always cook any dish I liked. Observing how she cooked motivated me to try cooking. Ten years later, I'm sharing with you my cooking inspiration as well as the reasons why I love it.

1.    Trying something different

Various cuisines of the world use different kinds of ingredients. You can download and share a lot of recipes on the internet. Even so, you can add your own unique twists to recipes and experiment with various versions and styles.

Trying out new recipes and ingredients isn't bad when cooking, as long as you produce something edible…

2.    Enjoyment

Whomever you cook for— family, friends, or even yourself—you'll surely have fun doing it. It's satisfying to see how the combination of various spices, meat, and vegetables yield an awesome flavor. From cutting to cooking them, the whole process is nothing but pure joy.

3.    Receiving wonderful feedback

Don't you get a sense of pride, joy, and accomplishment when people love the dish you've cooked and let you know their thoughts? You'll definitely savor the moment when you hear someone praise your cooking skills.

Each time someone tells me, "This has a great flavor" or "This is insanely delicious!" I get more motivated to become a better cook…

4.    Healthy eating

Rather than consuming processed food, using fresh ingredients for your dishes makes them good for the body. Cook your own meals so that you can add more fresh vegetables and fruits to your diet. Cooking also allows you to discover more about the different nutrients in your meals.

Because you prepare your meals yourself, having digestive problems will be the least of your worries…

5.    Therapeutic activity

Based on my experience, cooking calms the mind. Finding food in the fridge, gathering the ingredients, getting them ready, and assembling everything together to create a yummy dish are more relaxing than just spending idle time on the couch watching TV. Cooking never makes me stressed.

My mother would always tell me: Cooking is an edible way to make your loved ones feel loved…

Keeping Up Your Passion for Cooking

Cooking is not for everyone. But people who are passionate about cooking and their families are fortunate indeed. It spreads happiness around. Do you love cooking? Sustain your passion—it's the best feeling ever!

When combined with love, cooking feeds the soul…

From my unending love for cooking, I'm creating this book series and hoping to share my passion with all of you. With my many experiences of failures, I have created this book series and hopefully it helps you. This Ingredient Recipes Series covers these subjects:

- Cheese Recipes
- Butter Recipes
- Red Wine Recipes
- Cajun Spice Recipes
- Mayonnaise Recipes
- ...

I really appreciate that you have selected "Hello! 150 Wine Recipes" and for reading to the end. I anticipate that this book shall give you the source of strength during the times that you are really exhausted, as well as be your best friend in the comforts of your own home. Please also give me some love by sharing your own exciting cooking time in the comments segment below.

# List of Abbreviations

| C Ms. Mr. King | |
| :---: | :---: |
| **LIST OF ABBREVIATIONS** | |
| tbsp(s). | tablespoon(s) |
| tsp(s). | teaspoon(s) |
| c. | cup(s) |
| oz. | ounce(s) |
| lb(s). | pound(s) |

# 150 Amazing Wine Recipes

*** 

## 1.  3-ingredient Mussels With White Wine And Pesto

*"Made with just three ingredients besides the oil and seasoning, the scallops derive their flavor from the packaged pesto."*
*Serving: 4 appetizer servings | Prep: 10m*

## Ingredients

- 1 cup dry white wine
- 2 lbs. mussels, debearded, scrubbed
- 1/2 cup fresh store-bought pesto
- Kosher salt, freshly ground pepper

## Direction

- Place wine in a big pot and bring to a boil. Add mussels. Cover the pot and return to heat. When it starts to boil again, reduce heat to simmer and continue cooking for about 4 minutes or until mussels begin to open up. Add in the pesto, stir, and season with pepper and salt.
- Discarding the liquid, spoon the mussels into individual bowls topped with broth. Serve hot.

## Nutrition Information

- Calories: 557
- Total Carbohydrate: 13 g
- Cholesterol: 74 mg
- Total Fat: 39 g
- Fiber: 2 g
- Protein: 33 g

- Sodium: 1307 mg
- Saturated Fat: 7 g

## 2.  Artillery Punch

*"A simple punch with a simple syrup."*
*Serving: Makes 24 six-oz. servings*

## Ingredients

- 1 bottle (750 milliliters) rye whiskey
- 1 bottle (750 milliliters) red wine
- 25 oz. chilled strong tea
- 12 oz. dark rum
- 6 oz. gin
- 6 oz. brandy
- 1 oz. Bénédictine
- 12 oz. fresh orange juice
- 6 oz. fresh lemon juice
- 6 oz. simple syrup
- 1 large block of ice
- Lemon wheels, for garnish

## Direction

- In a big nonreactive bowl or pan, put in all the liquid ingredients; blend well and cover. Place in the refrigerator for 4hrs or more. In the middle of a big punch bowl, put ice and pour in punch. Garnish.

## Nutrition Information

- Calories: 198
- Total Carbohydrate: 8 g
- Total Fat: 0 g
- Fiber: 0 g
- Protein: 0 g
- Sodium: 4 mg
- Saturated Fat: 0 g

## 3. Asian Dipping Sauce

*"Use this sauce as a dressing for Asian salads or serve with lettuce wraps and spring rolls."*
*Serving: 10 | Prep: 10m | Ready in: 10m*

### Ingredients

- 1/2 cup water
- 1/4 cup white sugar
- 2 tbsps. soy sauce
- 2 tbsps. rice wine vinegar
- 2 tbsps. ketchup
- 1 tbsp. lemon juice
- 1 tsp. garlic and red chile paste, or more to taste
- 1/8 tsp. sesame oil

### Direction

- Dissolve the sugar in the water until sugar melts then stir in the rest of the ingredients: sesame oil, red chile paste, garlic, lemon juice, ketchup, rice wine vinegar and soy sauce. Mix until smooth. Cool in refrigerator before serving.

### Nutrition Information

- Calories: 26 calories;
- Total Carbohydrate: 6.1 g
- Cholesterol: 0 mg
- Total Fat: 0.1 g
- Protein: 0.3 g
- Sodium: 231 mg

## 4. Aunt Betsy's Favorite

*"There's almost nothing simpler and easier to make than this."*
*Serving: Makes about 12 servings.*

### Ingredients

- 1 bottle dry red wine
- 2 cups tawny or ruby port
- 1 cup brandy
- 8 cubes sugar
- Peel of 2 oranges
- 6 cloves
- 1 stick cinnamon

### Direction

- In a sturdy saucepan, combine all the ingredients and heat slowly without letting the mixture reach a simmering point. Prepare 4-oz. punch glasses.

## 5. Baked Risotto With Roasted Vegetables

*"This is the best way of making risotto if you don't like hovering around the food and until it's done. You can head off to do other things while it's cooking. When it's done, you'll have yourself a wonderful meal of velvety, warm risotto with roasted vegetables!"*
*Serving: Serves 2*

### Ingredients

- Roasted Winter Vegetables
- 1 tbsp extra-virgin olive oil
- 1/2 onion, finely chopped
- 3/4 cup/150 g Arborio rice
- 1/4 cup/60 ml dry white wine
- 2 to 2 1/4 cups/480 to 540 ml hot water, homemade or packaged organic chicken broth, or a mix
- 3/4 tsp kosher salt
- Pinch of freshly ground black pepper
- 1 to 2 tbsp unsalted butter
- 1/4 cup/30 g freshly grated Parmigiano-Reggiano cheese, plus more for garnish

### Direction

- Preheat the oven to Gas 6, 200°C or 400°F. Place the vegetables atop a single baking tray or sheet of the oven. (As for the risotto, it will be cooked on the rack at the bottom).
- Meanwhile, pour olive oil into a Dutch oven or an ovenproof saucepan and heat it up at a moderately high heat. Insert onion. Stir and

cook for around 3 minutes until the onion softens and turns semitransparent. Insert the rice and keep mixing in the oil until it is coated. Pour wine and stir for another minute until the wine evaporates. Add pepper, salt and 480ml of hot water. Let it boil and cover it up before moving it into the oven. When there's 25 minutes left before the vegetables are done, bake on the bottom rack. Take a look at the risotto when the 25 minutes, check risotto. Majority of the liquid has seeped into it and rice is cooked. Get the risotto out of the oven and mix cheese, butter and stir in another 120ml 1/2 cup of hot cups water into it. Before serving, top it with thin shavings of Parmigiano-Reggiano and roasted vegetables (try a combination of tomato, yellow onion and winter squash).

## 6. Baked Shrimp Toasts

*"A good old shrimp toast can brighten up any seafood lover's day."*
*Serving: Makes 32 hors d'oeuvres*

### Ingredients

- 4 tsps. minced garlic
- 1 tbsp. minced peeled fresh ginger
- 1 tbsp. vegetable oil
- 1 tbsp. mirin*
- 2 tsps. soy sauce
- 1/2 tsp. salt
- 3/4 lb. medium shrimp in shell (31 to 35 per lb.), peeled, deveined, and cut into 1/2-inch pieces
- 3 tbsps. chopped fresh cilantro
- 1 (9- by 4-inch) white Pullman loaf, unsliced

### Direction

- In a heavy 8- to 9-inch skillet, cook and stir ginger and garlic in oil over moderate heat for 1 minute until they're fragrant and soft. Stir the salt, soy sauce and mirin in and let it simmer for 15 seconds (omit sauce if making ahead; see cook's note below). Pour the marinade into a bowl and let it cool down to room temperature.
- Mix the cilantro and shrimp in, tossing to marinate and coat. Cover and keep chilled for 1 hour.
- Put oven rack in upper third of oven and preheat oven to 350 degrees F.
- Turn bread load onto its side, use a long serrated knife to cut the crusts evenly from the bottom and discard. Slice the bread from the bottom into a 3/8-inch thick slice, trimming the crusts from the sides. On a baking sheet, place a slice of bread and bake until it turns dry but not colored or for 8 minutes total. Keep the remainder of the loaf for another use. Leaving the bread on the baking sheet, move it away from the oven.
- Increase quickly the oven temperature at once to 475°F.
- Spread all of the shrimp mixture onto the entire surface, covering it entirely, of hot toast packing it down in a thick, even layer. When the oven temperature is at 475°F, bake the shrimp toast for 12 to 15 minutes or until the topping is thoroughly cooked. Use a big, flat spatula to transfer the toast onto a rack to cool for 5 minutes before moving it to a cutting board.
- Use an extremely sharp knife to halve the shrimp toast crosswise and cut each of the half lengthwise into four strips making 8 strips total. Cut each strip up further into another 4 pieces. Serve the toasts warm or at room temperature.
- Cooks' note: Shrimp can be marinated (without salt in marinade) up to 4 hours. Stir in salt before proceeding.

### Nutrition Information

- Calories: 15
- Total Carbohydrate: 1 g
- Cholesterol: 13 mg
- Total Fat: 1 g
- Fiber: 0 g
- Protein: 2 g
- Sodium: 83 mg

- Saturated Fat: 0 g

## 7. Beaumes-de-venise Cake With Grapes

*"Gateau De Beaumes-De-Venise Aux Raisins – this name was derived from a town in the Vaucluse and inspired by the lovely wine from the area."*
*Serving: Serves 10*

### Ingredients

- Olive oil
- 1 1/2 cups all purpose flour
- 1 tsp. baking powder
- 1 tsp. salt
- 1/4 tsp. baking soda
- 3/4 cup plus 2 tbsps. sugar
- 8 tbsps. (1 stick) unsalted butter, room temperature
- 3 tbsps. extra-virgin olive oil
- 2 large eggs
- 1 tsp. grated lemon peel
- 1 tsp. grated orange peel
- 1 tsp. vanilla extract
- 1 cup Beaumes-de-Venise or other Muscat wine
- 1 1/2 cups red seedless grapes

### Direction

- Preheat the oven to 400°F. Layer olive oil over the 10-inch diameter springform pan then use parchment to line the pan's bottom and brush olive oil over parchment.
- In a bowl, sift the next 3 ingredients and flour in. In a big bowl, whisk 3 tbsps. of oil, 6 tbsps. of butter and 3/4 cups of sugar until smooth. Beat vanilla, both peel and eggs. In an alternating manner, add the flour mixture followed by the wine in 3 additions each. After every addition, whisk the mixture until just smooth. Move the batter to prepped pan and smooth the top. Scatter grapes over the batter and bake the cake for 20 minutes until the top is set. Use 2 tbsps. of butter to dot the top of

the cake. Scatter 2 tbsps. of sugar over the cake and bake for another 20 minutes. It is ready when it turns golden and when an inserted tester is pulled out from the middle completely clean. Let it cool on rack for 20 minutes in the pan, releasing the pan sides. Serve at room temperature, slightly warm.

### Nutrition Information

- Calories: 318
- Total Carbohydrate: 37 g
- Cholesterol: 62 mg
- Total Fat: 16 g
- Fiber: 1 g
- Protein: 3 g
- Sodium: 258 mg
- Saturated Fat: 7 g

## 8. Beef And Potato Supper Pot

*"Enjoy this simple dish on cold winter nights. Aside from beef, you can also use chicken or pork."*
*Serving: Makes 4 to 6 servings*

### Ingredients

- 1 tbsp. vegetable oil
- 3 medium potatoes (about 1 3/4 lbs.), peeled and cut into bite-size chunks
- 2 medium onions, peeled and coarsely chopped
- 1/3 lb. lean beef, sliced into thin bite-size strips
- 1 2/3 cups dashi
- 3 tbsps. sugar
- 3 tbsps. sake
- 3 tbsps. soy sauce
- 1 tbsp. mirin

### Direction

- On medium heat, heat oil in a big shallow pot; add beef, onions, and potatoes. Sauté for 5mins. Mix in mirin, dashi, soy sauce, sugar, and sake. Turn to low heat and cook for 25-

30mins while slightly covered until the potatoes fall apart and melt into the sauce.

## 9. Berry Rosé Sangria

*Serving: Makes 6 to 8 drinks | Prep: 10m*

### Ingredients

- 1/2 cup sugar
- 1 cup water
- 1/4 cup crème de cassis
- 1 1/2 cups assorted berries such as blackberries, blueberries, and raspberries
- 1 (750-ml) bottle chilled dry rosé wine
- 2 tsps. fresh lemon juice, or to taste

### Direction

- In a heatproof pitcher, put in berries. In a small pot, simmer crème de cassis, water, and sugar; stir until the sugar dissolves. In the heatproof pitcher, pour in syrup and set aside for 5mins; stir in lemon juice and wine and mix well. Refrigerate while covered until ready to use. Serve sangria with ice.
- It can last up to three days when covered in the refrigerator.

## 10. Black Cod With Miso

*"Baked black cod that is soaked in sweet Nobu-style Saikyo miso."*
*Serving: Makes 4 servings*

### Ingredients

- saké
- 3/4 cup (150 ml) mirin
- 2 cups (450 g) white miso paste
- 1 1/4 cups (225 g) granulated sugar
- 4 black cod fillets, about 1/2 lb. (230 g) each
- 3 cups (800 g) Nobu-style Saikyo Miso
- 1 stalk hajikami per serving

### Direction

- To prepare the miso, boil mirin and sake on high heat in a medium pot for 20secs until the alcohol evaporates.
- Turn to low heat and put in the miso paste; use a wooden spoon to mix. Once the miso dissolves fully, turn to high heat and put in sugar. Using a wooden spoon, stir the mixture regularly to prevent the bottom from burning. Take off heat when the sugar dissolves completely. Let the mixture cool to room temperature.
- Prepare the cod. Use paper towels to pat dry fillets thoroughly. Spread Nobu-style Saikyo Miso over the fish. Arrange fish in a non-reactive bowl or dish; use plastic wrap to cover it firmly. Refrigerate and let soak for 2-3 days.
- Preheat the oven to 200 degrees C gas 6 or 400 degrees F. Gently wipe off extra miso on the fish but avoid rinsing it off completely. Broil or grill fillets until the surface is brown then bake in the oven for 10-15mins.
- Put fillets on plates and add hajikami on top. Drop extra miso on every plate.

## 11. Border Punch

*Serving: Makes about 25 servings.*

### Ingredients

- 2 quarts Scotch whisky
- 1 quart ginger wine
- 3 tbsps. honey
- Juice of 4 oranges
- Peel of two oranges, cut into spirals and studded with cloves

### Direction

- Combine honey, ginger wine, orange peel, orange juice, and Scotch whiskey in a large saucepan. Heat the mixture, making sure not to boil it. Pour this punch into 4-oz. mugs.

Garnish each mug with a strip of clove-studded peel.

## 12. Braised Chicken Marsala

*Serving: Serves 4*

### Ingredients

- 4 skin-on, bone-in chicken thighs (about 1 1/4 lbs.)
- 4 chicken drumsticks (about 1 lb.)
- Coarse salt and freshly ground pepper
- 1 tbsp. extra-virgin olive oil
- 2 red onions, peeled and quartered through the stem
- 2 plum tomatoes, cut into 1-inch pieces
- 6 sprigs thyme
- 3/4 cup Marsala (sweet Italian fortified wine)
- 1 1/4 cups chicken stock, homemade or low-sodium store-bought
- Sage Polenta

### Direction

- Heat oven to 400 degrees F. Wash chicken and use a paper towel to pat dry. Sprinkle pepper and salt on each side to season. On medium-high heat, place a high-sided big skillet and add oil to heat. Place chicken in batches into the skillet and cook until both sides are browned, flipping once for 10-12 minutes. Place chicken into a platter and using a parchment paper tent chicken loosely. Wrap with foil after to keep chicken warm. Spill off the excess fat after all the chicken turns brown.
- Toss in tomatoes, thyme, and onions into the pan. Cook, mixing occasionally for about 4 minutes until golden brown. Add in Marsala and cook until liquid is reduced in half for about 5 minutes. Place the chicken again into the pan and add in the stock, allow simmering. Place into the oven and bake until chicken is thoroughly cooked and tender for about 35 minutes. Prepare a platter to transfer chicken. Cover to keep chicken warm.

- Remove excess fat in the pan by skimming. On medium-high heat, allow simmering until liquid thickens slightly for about 5 minutes. Prepare shallow bowls and distribute polenta. Put chicken over and scoop sauce of pan on top of each bowl. Serve.

## 13. Braised Short Ribs With Dijon Mustard

*"The best ribs to use for this recipe are the short ones as they're great on flavor. Serve the ribs with roasted or mashed potatoes. The dish takes about three hours to make."*
*Serving: Makes 4 servings | Prep: 45m*

### Ingredients

- 4 cups dry red wine
- 4 lb beef short ribs (also called flanken)
- 10 shallots (10 oz), trimmed, halved if large
- 3 tbsps. coarse-grain Dijon mustard, or to taste
- 6 plum tomatoes, halved lengthwise

### Direction

- Place wine in a medium sized (2 quart) heavy saucepan and boil until it reduces to one cup.
- Separately, cut towel dried ribs crosswise in pieces 2 1/2 inches long. Season generously with pepper and salt.
- Heat a (5 quart) heavy, dry saucepan on high heat and brown ribs for 8 minutes in small batches. Remove from heat and transfer ribs to a bowl using tongs.
- Reduce heat and cook the shallots on medium heat, stirring all the time. When browned, transfer using a slotter spoon to another bowl.
- Pour the wine and mustard into the pot and add the ribs. Cover pot and allow to simmer for about 1 3/4 hours.
- Stir in the tomatoes and shallots gently, cover pot and allow to simmer for 40 minutes or until the meat is tender.
- Carefully lift the ribs, tomatoes and shallots from pan and transfer on a serving platter.

Skim off fat from the liquid, season to taste with mustard, salt and pepper and pour on the ribs.

## Nutrition Information

- Calories: 1953
- Total Carbohydrate: 19 g
- Cholesterol: 345 mg
- Total Fat: 165 g
- Fiber: 4 g
- Protein: 68 g
- Sodium: 364 mg
- Saturated Fat: 72 g

## 14. Braised Veal Shanks

*"This veal recipe can serve four as a main course or eight as a Pastitsio."*
*Serving: Makes 4 to 8 servings | Prep: 45m*

## Ingredients

- 8 (12- to 14-oz) meaty cross-cut veal shanks (also known as ossobuco; each about 13/4 inches thick)
- 3/4 cup all-purpose flour
- 3 1/2 tsps. salt
- 1 1/4 tsps. black pepper
- 6 tbsps. extra-virgin olive oil
- 1 large onion, chopped (2 cups)
- 4 large garlic cloves, finely chopped
- 5 anchovy fillets, rinsed, patted dry, and finely chopped
- 2 Turkish bay leaves or 1 California
- 1 cup dry white wine
- 1 (28-oz) can whole tomatoes in juice, pulsed (including juice) in food processor until chopped
- 1 cup water
- 2 (4- by 1-inch) strips fresh lemon zest
- 2 (4- by 1-inch) strips fresh orange zest
- 1/4 cup finely chopped fresh flat-leaf parsley
- 1 tsp. finely grated fresh lemon zest
- 1 tsp. finely grated fresh orange zest
- 1 large garlic clove, minced

## Direction

- Prepare the shanks. Place the rack in the middle of the oven; preheat to 350 degrees F.
- Pat dry shanks. On a sheet of wax paper, combine a tsp. pepper, 2tsp salt, and flour. On medium-high heat, heat 2tbsp oil in a 12-in heavy pan until hot although not smoking. Meanwhile, roll four shanks in the flour mix; shake off the excess mixture. Cook shanks for 8-10mins until all sides are brown, use tongs to flip shanks. Move to a big roasting pan measuring 17x12x2-in. Put 2tbsp oil in the pan and cook the remaining shanks. Get rid of the leftover flour mixture.
- Put leftover 2tbsp oil in the pan. On medium heat, cook and stir bay leaves, remaining quarter pepper, onion, half tsp. salt, anchovies, and garlic for 6-8mins until the onion is soft. Pour in wine then boil for 2mins until it reduces by 1/2 while scraping the base of the pot to remove the brown bits. Mix in leftover tsp. of salt, tomatoes, zest strips, and water; boil. Pour in mixture on shanks and use a sheet of foil to cover pan tightly; braise for an hour in the oven. Flip shanks, cover, and keep on braising for another 1 1/2hr until the meat is very tender.
- Take it out of the oven and scoop out the fat on the sauce surface. Move shanks with the sauce on a big platter; remove bay leaves.
- Prepare the gremolata. Combine garlic, grated zest, and parley; rub the mixture on shanks.
- Veal shanks can be prepared two days in advance. Let it cool in the sauce without cover then refrigerate while covered. Place in a 425 degrees F oven for 40mins. To make pastitsio, keep four braised shanks, 1/2 of gremolata, and four cups sauce. Slice meat into one-inch portions and mix into the gremolata with the saved sauce. Let it cool without cover then refrigerate covered.

## Nutrition Information

- Calories: 653
- Total Carbohydrate: 25 g
- Cholesterol: 264 mg

- Total Fat: 27 g
- Fiber: 5 g
- Protein: 72 g
- Sodium: 1852 mg
- Saturated Fat: 6 g

## 15. Campari Spritz

*"Colorful and fancy Campari drink with a citrusy flavor.*
*The perfect cocktail for your party!"*
*Serving: Makes 1*

### Ingredients

- 2 oz. Campari
- 3 oz. dry rosé
- Splash of lemon soda
- 1 lemon wheel

### Direction

- Fill the rock glass with ice and pour rosé and Campari. Add soda over and slowly swirl to blend. Mix in the lemon wheel.

## 16. Champagne Punch With Ginger, Lemon, And Sage

*"Feel refreshed with a tasty punch with a sparkling appearance. Have a sip!"*
*Serving: 20 servings | Prep: 20m*

### Ingredients

- 1 lemon, thinly sliced
- 3–4 sprigs sage
- 8 strips lemon zest (from 1 lemon)
- 1/2 large bunch of sage
- 1/2 cup sugar
- 1 1/4 cups fresh lemon juice
- 2 cups gin
- 2 cups ginger liqueur, such as Canton
- 6 cups unflavored sparkling water
- 2 bottles chilled sparkling wine

- A Bundt or tube pan; a large (about 6-quart) punch bowl or mixing bowl

### Direction

- Preparation for ice ring: In a Bundt pan, put the sage and lemon slices at the bottom. Pour cold water to fill pan leaving about 1–inch gap above. Keep in freezer until settled for at least 6 hours and up to overnight.
- Preparation for punch: In a measuring cup, muddle the sage, sugar, and lemon zest with a pour spout until sugar turns to green. Pour 2 cups of warm water. Mix until sugar melts. Set aside for 10 minutes, allowing the punch to infuse.
- Add in lemon juice; mix. Using a fine-mesh sieve, strain punches into a big punch bowl. Add in ginger liqueur and gin; mix.
- To serve: Prepare a hot bowl of water to dip the bottom of the Bundt pan. Prepare a plate on top of a mold, turn over ice ring to the plate then pour into the punch bowl. Add in the wine and sparkling water. Gently mix.
- Punch can be done 2 days ahead without the wine and sparkling water. Store in a sealed container and keep in the chiller.

## 17. Cheese Fondue With Beer And Bourbon

*"This delicious fondue feature Babybel cheese that complements the Gruyere and keeps the mixture intact."*
*Serving: Serves 4*

### Ingredients

- 2 garlic cloves, halved lengthwise
- 1/2 cup Belgian beer (such as Duvel)
- 2 cups dry white wine, divided
- 3 tbsps. cornstarch
- 1 lb. Gruyère, coarsely grated
- 1 lb. Babybel cheese, grated
- 2 tbsps. bourbon or brandy
- 1/4 tsp. baking soda
- 1 tbsp. fresh lemon juice

- Kosher salt
- 4 cups (1-inch pieces) country-style bread, preferably day-old
- Assorted ham and salumi, pickles, and crudités (for serving)

## Direction

- Spread cut sides of garlic inside a big pot; finely grate garlic into the pot. On medium heat, pour in and boil 1 1/2 cup wine and beer. Stir leftover half cup of wine and cornstarch together in a small bowl until there are no lumps; incorporate the mixture into the pot. Boil while stirring regularly then lower heat to maintain a low simmer. Gradually put in Babybel and Gruyere; stir until smooth. Make sure to fully blend each batch of cheese before mixing another batch.
- In a small bowl, combine baking soda and bourbon. Stir the mixture into the fondue; add salt and lemon juice. Move the mixture on a fondue pot. Serve with crudités, bread, pickles, ham, and salumi to dip.

## Nutrition Information

- Calories: 1122
- Total Carbohydrate: 35 g
- Cholesterol: 229 mg
- Total Fat: 70 g
- Fiber: 2 g
- Protein: 69 g
- Sodium: 1177 mg
- Saturated Fat: 42 g

## 18. Cherries In Spiced Wine Syrup

*"These delicious cherries are best enjoyed with lb. cake or ice cream. You can also eat it with biscotti or whipped cream."*
*Serving: Makes 4 servings | Prep: 20m*

## Ingredients

- 1 Turkish or 1/2 California bay leaf
- 4 whole cloves
- 4 black peppercorns
- 3 (3- by 1/2-inch) strips fresh lemon zest
- 1 1/2 cups red Zinfandel
- 1/2 cup kirsch or other cherry-flavored brandy
- 1/2 cup water
- 1/2 cup sugar
- 3 cups fresh or frozen (not thawed) pitted sour cherries (1 lb)
- 1 (3-inch) cinnamon stick
- 1 vanilla bean, halved lengthwise
- kitchen string; a 4-inch square of cheesecloth; a 1-qt jar with lid

## Direction

- In a cheesecloth bag, put in zest, bay leaf, peppercorns, and cloves; tie together.
- In a 4qt heavy pot, mix the cheesecloth bag, Zinfandel, sugar, kirsch, and water together; boil. Put in vanilla bean, frozen or fresh cherries with the juices and cinnamon stick. Let it simmer without cover for 3-4mins until the cherries are tender while still maintaining their shape.
- Drain and sieve cherries on a bowl. Put the cooking liquid back in the pan with the cheesecloth bag, vanilla bean, and cinnamon stick. Boil for 12mins until it reduces to 1 1/4 cup. Let the liquid cool for a bit; remove the cheesecloth bag, cinnamon stick, and vanilla bean. Move the liquid and cherries on a jar and cover; let it chill for at least two hours to bring out the flavors.
- It can last for a month when stored in a jar and refrigerated.

## Nutrition Information

- Calories: 303
- Total Carbohydrate: 43 g
- Total Fat: 0 g
- Fiber: 2 g
- Protein: 1 g
- Sodium: 6 mg
- Saturated Fat: 0 g

# 19. Chicken Liver Mousse With Riesling-thyme Gelée

*"You can add a wine topping on top of the lovely mousse if you wish to for some extra fun. Treat your family, friends and guests to a delectable, flavourful indulgence!"*
*Serving: Makes 3 cups*

## Ingredients

- 1 lb. chicken livers, cleaned
- 4 cups milk, divided
- 2 cups (4 sticks) unsalted butter, room temperature, divided
- 3 tbsps. finely chopped shallots
- 3 sprigs thyme
- 2 tbsps. Calvados (apple brandy)
- 2 tsps. kosher salt plus more
- 1/2 tsp. freshly ground black pepper
- 1 tsp. unflavored gelatin
- 2 tsps. sugar
- 3/4 cup sweet (Auslese) Riesling
- Fresh thyme sprigs or leaves (optional)
- 16 1/4"-thick slices white sandwich bread, each cut into 4 triangles
- Melted unsalted butter
- Small (2-4-oz.) glass jars or bowls

## Direction

- Pour 2 cups of milk into a glass bowl and soak the chicken livers inside to tone down the flavors. Put a lid on. For the next 2 hours, let it chill before draining it and discarding the milk. Insert the livers back into the same bowl before adding the 2 remaining cups of milk. Put a lid on and let it chill for 2 hours or through the night. Drain the milk and discard it. Cleanse the livers with water and use paper towels to dry them by patting.
- On top of a midsize bowl, place a fine-mesh strainer over it and put it to one side.
- Over a moderately low heat, heat 2 tbsps. of butter in a big skillet until melted. Insert the thyme and shallots. For around 10 minutes, stir occasionally and cook until they soften immensely. Place the livers in and turn the heat up to medium. Cook for 4 minutes until the livers are firm while maintaining the pink on the inside. During the cooking process, flip it over one time. Move the pan away from the heat before mixing in the Calvados. Place it back on the heat. Cook for around 30 seconds until the Calvados reduces into half. Get rid of the thyme.
- Process the liver mixture inside of a food processor with 2 tsps. of pepper and salt until it smoothens out. During the processing period, insert the remainder of the butter by tablespoonfuls until all of it is mixed together well. Move the mousse to a prepped strainer. Crush the mousse through the strainer with a rubber spatula. Rinse and dry the strainer before straining the mousse once more. Get rid of the solids left on the strainer. In little jars, distribute the mousse. For 1 to 2 hours, let the mousse chill until they firm up.
- For gelee and toasts: In a midsized microwave-safe bowl, pour in 1/4 cup of water and scatter gelatine atop it. For approximately 10 minutes, leave it standing until it softens. For around 30 seconds, microwave the gelatine mixture. It should turn clear after it has dissolved in the microwave. Mix in the sugar, stirring until it dissolves before mixing the wine in.
- Get some of the gelée with a spoon to set over the mousse in jars, creating a layer about 1/4 inches. There may be some gelée left over. If desired, place thyme sprigs or leaves atop every jar. Use plastic wrap to cover it up and keep it in the fridge for an hour until the gelée sets. If desired, prepare these 3 days in advance. Just remember to store it in the refrigerator.
- Preheat the oven to 450°F. Prepare a rimmed baking sheet to place the bread triangles on. Apply the melted butter. For around 5 minutes, bake them until they turn a golden brown. If desired, bake one day in advance. When done baking, keep it airtight at room temperate. When ready to serve toasts, make sure to leave the mousse for half an hour at room temperature first to allow it to soften a little.

## Nutrition Information

- Calories: 280
- Total Carbohydrate: 14 g
- Cholesterol: 123 mg
- Total Fat: 21 g
- Fiber: 1 g
- Protein: 7 g
- Sodium: 279 mg
- Saturated Fat: 13 g

## 20. Chicken Sauté With White Wine

*"You can vary the flavor for this basic chicken sauté recipe. You can also use flour to dredge the chicken for a browner colour. However unflavored chicken is known to be more delicate in taste."*
*Serving: Serves 4*

## Ingredients

- 3 1/2 to 4 lb. chicken, quartered
- Flour (optional)
- 4-6 tbsps. butter
- Salt, freshly ground pepper
- 1 cup white wine (Pouilly Fuissé or White Pinot)
- Garnish: chopped parsley or chives

## Direction

- Heat butter in a skillet and brown the chicken pieces. Turn each piece so it colors evenly. Season with pepper and salt. Add white wine (about 1/2 - 3/4 cup). Reduce heat, cover the pan and allow to cook until chicken becomes tender. Add any other desired flavorings while cooking. Turn the chicken pieces a couple of times to absorb the flavorings and the juices. When cooked and tender, transfer the chicken to a warmed platter. Add a little wine into the pan and allow it to cook along with the juices. After the juices have cooked for several minutes, pour on the chicken and serve garnished with chives or parsley or as desired.

- Serve with any one of these wines: White Pinot, Meursault or Pouilly Fuisse.

## Nutrition Information

- Calories: 1072
- Total Carbohydrate: 1 g
- Cholesterol: 357 mg
- Total Fat: 78 g
- Protein: 79 g
- Sodium: 1116 mg
- Saturated Fat: 27 g

## 21. Chicken Scallopine With Hazelnut-cream Sauce

*"This dish is tied together with Madeira's nutty flavors and lovely, crunchy hazelnut."*
*Serving: Makes 4 servings*

## Ingredients

- 2 skinless boneless chicken breast halves
- 1 tbsp. butter
- 1 tbsp. canola oil
- 1 large shallot, minced (about 1/4 cup)
- 1/4 cup Madeira
- 1/3 cup heavy whipping cream
- 1/4 cup hazelnuts, toasted , husked, chopped (about 1 1/4 oz.)

## Direction

- Detach the tenderloins from the chicken breast halves then cut each chicken breast on half diagonally into 4 smaller pieces. In between of 2 pieces of plastic wrap or waxed paper, set the tenderloins and cutlets down. Use a mallet to smack each piece until it's about 1/3-inch thick. Sprinkle pepper and salt onto both sides of the pounded chicken. Over moderately high heat, melt butter in oil inside of a big, sturdy skillet. Work in batches, add chicken to the skillet and stir until they are thoroughly cooked and lightly browned, about 1-1/2 minutes on each side. Move the chicken to a plate and cover it up to make sure it stays warm. In the same skillet, sauté shallots for 3 minutes until they turn tender then pour the Madeira in. Bring it to a boil and stir to remove any browned bits. After adding the cream, leave it boiling for 2 minutes until the sauce thickens a little. Insert the hazelnut and season the sauce with pepper and salt. Before serving, pour this sauce over the chicken.

## Nutrition Information

- Calories: 329
- Total Carbohydrate: 6 g
- Cholesterol: 99 mg
- Total Fat: 29 g
- Fiber: 1 g
- Protein: 13 g
- Sodium: 35 mg
- Saturated Fat: 12 g

## 22. Chicken With Chestnuts

*"Northern China, or sometimes Shanghai, use Chinese chestnuts in their food. They are used in almost any casseroles and braised dishes. It will take you about 1 hour in total to prepare and cook this yummy dish."*
*Serving: Makes 4 servings (as part of a Chinese meal)*

## Ingredients

- 3 tbsps. coarsely crushed yellow rock sugar (sometimes labeled "yellow rock candy")
- 3 tbsps. Chinese rice wine (preferably Shaoxing) or medium-dry Sherry
- 2 tbsps. dark mushroom soy sauce
- 1/2 tbsp. oyster sauce
- 2 cups water
- 2 1/4 lbs. whole chicken legs (including thighs; about 2 large)
- 2 tbsps. vegetable oil
- 1 (1-inch) piece fresh ginger, peeled and cut crosswise into 1/8-inch-thick slices
- 1 large garlic clove, smashed
- 16 frozen shelled and blanched chestnuts (3 oz.), thawed

- 1 tsp. Asian sesame oil
- 2 tbsps. chopped scallion

## Direction

- In a medium-sized bowl, combine and mix oyster sauce, soy sauce, water, wine and sugar together and put aside.
- Use a meat cleaver to cut the chicken to create 1-inch pieces through the bones. Put the cut chicken into a 4-quart pot full of boiling water then let it simmer for 5 minutes without cover. Drain the cooked chicken in a colander and remove the skin, tiny bone shards and excess fat once the chicken is cool enough to touch.
- Heat a wok with vegetable oil on moderately high heat until hot but not smoking and stir-fry the garlic and ginger for 1-2 minutes until golden then use a slotted spoon to put the stir-fried garlic and ginger on a plate. Put in 1/2 of the chicken into the same wok and stir-fry for 2 minutes or until golden in color then put the cooked chicken onto the same plate as the stir-fried garlic and ginger. Stir-fry the leftover 1/2 of the chicken with chestnuts for about 2 minutes until the chicken is golden in color. Put the cooked chicken and stir-fried garlic and ginger back into the wok then mix in the soy mixture. Cover the wok and let the chicken cook on moderate heat for 25 minutes or until the sauce has reduced by half. Remove the cover and continue to cook the mixture over moderately high heat while stirring often for 5-10 minutes or until the sauce is thick in consistency and has coated the chicken evenly. Remove the wok from heat and mix in the sesame oil. Finish off with a sprinkle of scallions on top then serve.

## Nutrition Information

- Calories: 724
- Total Carbohydrate: 23 g
- Cholesterol: 237 mg
- Total Fat: 49 g
- Fiber: 0 g
- Protein: 43 g
- Sodium: 723 mg

- Saturated Fat: 12 g

## 23. Citrus Terrine With Candied Grapefruit Strips

*"This warm little fruity treat is great for family and friend hangouts."*

### Ingredients

- 2 large red grapefruits
- 1 large white grapefruit
- 2 navel oranges
- 2 tangerines
- 1 tablespooncandied grapefruit strips 4 tsps. unflavored gelatin (less than 2 envelopes)
- 1/2 cup plus 3 tbsps. cold water
- 1 1/4 cups Orange Muscat such as Essensia
- 1/2 cup sugar

### Direction

- Use a sharp knife to cut all white pith and peel from the fruits before slicing pieces free from the membranes. Cut the candied grapefruit up into strips. In a loaf pan or a nonreactive terrine about 1-quart in size, decorate both the candied grapefruit and the fruit sections.
- Scatter gelatine over 3 tbsps. of cold water in a cup and give it about 1 minute to soften. Boil and stir sugar with Muscat in a small saucepan for 2 minutes until the sugar dissolves. Move the pan away from the heat and whisk the gelatine mixture until it dissolves. Pour the remaining cup of water in before transferring the mixture to a bowl that is placed inside of a bigger bowl filled with cold water and ice. Let the mixture cool down slightly, stirring it from time to time. Dispense the mixture out slowly over the fruit. Leave the terrine to chill with a cover on until it firms up for a minimum of 4 hours up to 2 full days. Dunk a slim knife into hot water before running the knife around the edges of the loaf pan or terrine. For 3 to 5 seconds, place the loaf pan or terrine inside of

a bigger pan filled with hot water to loosen it up. Prepare a serving plate and invert the content of the terrine or loaf pan onto the plate.

## 24. Clam Toasts With Pancetta

*"The salty-sweet pancetta soffritto is the cornerstone of this clam toast. I realized that pork and shellfish are a powerful duo!"*
*Serving: 2 servings*

### Ingredients

- 4 tbsps. olive oil, divided, plus more for drizzling
- 2 oz. pancetta (Italian bacon), finely chopped
- 4 garlic cloves, 2 thinly sliced, 2 whole
- 1/2 medium sweet onion, finely chopped
- 1/2 small fennel bulb, finely chopped, plus 1/4 cup fennel fronds
- 2 wide 3-inch strips lemon zest
- 1 bay leaf
- 1/2 tsp. ground fennel
- 1 cup dry white wine, divided
- 2 (1 1/12-inch-thick) slices sourdough bread
- 1 lb. Manila or littleneck clams or cockles
- 1/4 cup parsley leaves with tender stems

### Direction

- Put 1 tbsp. of oil in a large skillet and heat it over medium heat. Add the pancetta and cook for 5-7 minutes, stirring occasionally until crisp and brown. Add the sliced garlic and cook for 1 minute, stirring frequently until the edges of the garlic are golden. Adjust the heat to medium-low. Add the chopped fennel and sweet onion. Cook for 6-8 minutes, stirring occasionally until the onion is translucent and softened. Add a pinch of salt, ground fennel, a 1/2 cup of wine, lemon zest, and bay leaf. Adjust the heat to medium-high. Cook for 3 more minutes, stirring occasionally until the mixture is still saucy and the wine is mostly reduced. Transfer the soffritto into a medium bowl, discarding the bay leaf and lemon zest. Wipe the skillet out.

- Heat 2 tbsp. of oil over medium in the same skillet. Place the bread slices and cook each side for 1 minute until golden brown. Transfer into paper towels to drain. Cut a garlic clove in half and rub with the cut side of garlic on one side of each toast. Wipe the skillet out.
- Heat 1 tbsp. of oil over medium in the same skillet. Use the side of a chef's knife to crush the remaining garlic clove. Cook for 1 minute, stirring frequently until it starts to turn golden. Add the soffritto, a 1/2 cup of wine, and clams. Adjust the heat to medium-high. Bring the mixture to boil. Cook for 5-7 more minutes, uncovered until the liquid is reduced by half and the clams are already open (discard those who did not open). Add the fennel fronds and parsley. Cook for 1 minute more. Season it with salt according to your taste.
- Before serving, place the fried bread on plates and spoon clam mixture and cooked broth over. Drizzle over the oil and sprinkle the red pepper flakes.
- DO AHEAD: The soffritto can be prepared 2 days ahead. Just let it cool and keep it covered and chilled.

## Nutrition Information

- Calories: 1975
- Total Carbohydrate: 273 g
- Cholesterol: 87 mg
- Total Fat: 52 g
- Fiber: 14 g
- Protein: 91 g
- Sodium: 4485 mg
- Saturated Fat: 11 g

## 25. Clams Grilled In A Foil Pouch

*"Enjoy this dish at your backyard grill party! Grilled clams will make your party more FUN."*
*Serving: Serves 4 to 6*

## Ingredients

- 18 littleneck clams, scrubbed
- 2 diced seeded plum tomatoes
- 1 shallot, thinly sliced
- Leaves from a few sprigs of flat-leaf parsley and oregano sprigs, coarsely chopped
- A pinch of red pepper flakes
- 1 tbsp. unsalted butter (optional)
- 1/4 cup dry white wine

## Direction

- Prepare two pieces of 2 1/2 foot long heavy-duty aluminum foil. Then bundle at the middle, 18 scrubbed littleneck clams, 1 thinly chopped shallot, 2 diced plum tomatoes, seeded, and leaves from the coarsely chopped sprigs of parsley and sprigs of oregano. Put a pinch of red pepper flakes, if desired. Optional: add on top 1 tbsp. of unsalted butter. Form foil into a pouch by folding the sides.
- Add a 1/4 cup of dry white wine into the clam mixture. Tightly seal by rolling top edges several times. Leave a lot of space for clams to steam.
- Put pouch on the heated grill. Roast until shells will open for 12-15 minutes. Quickly serve alongside crusty grilled bread.

## Nutrition Information

- Calories: 80
- Total Carbohydrate: 6 g
- Cholesterol: 20 mg
- Total Fat: 1 g
- Fiber: 1 g
- Protein: 10 g
- Sodium: 396 mg
- Saturated Fat: 0 g

## 26. Claret Cobbler

*"A sip of simplicity."*
*Serving: Serves 1.*

### Ingredients

- Crushed ice
- Dash maraschino
- 1 tsp. superfine sugar
- 1 tsp. lemon juice
- 4 oz. claret
- Orange slice
- Pineapple stick

### Direction

- Put crushed ice into a tumbler until it's filled halfway. Stir in lemon juice, sugar and maraschino before pouring the claret in. Garnish with pineapple and orange.

## 27. Claret Cup

*"If you try searching, there are endless recipes, but simplicity wins for us. The best thing is that you can really just use any type of red wine and it'll work. You don't need to spend too much time thinking about it, just give it a shot and experiment to see what you end up enjoying the most."*
*Serving: Makes 1 cocktail | Prep: 5m*

### Ingredients

- 3 oz. red wine
- 1/2 oz. sherry (preferably Amontillado) or sweet vermouth
- 1/2 oz. orange curaçao (or triple sec if you like it sweeter)
- 1/2 oz. fresh lemon juice
- 2 oz. soda water
- Cucumber slices, for garnish
- Orange slices, for garnish

### Direction

- Prepare all the ingredients with the exception of the soda. Stir them together with ice. Over a highball glass full of ice, strain the mixture in.

Pour in the soda. Add orange slices and cucumber to garnish in the glass.

### Nutrition Information

- Calories: 130
- Total Carbohydrate: 8 g
- Total Fat: 0 g
- Fiber: 0 g
- Protein: 0 g
- Sodium: 17 mg
- Saturated Fat: 0 g

## 28. Claret Punch

*"Minimal ingredients and prep time for a spunky drink!"*
*Serving: Makes about 46 servings.*

### Ingredients

- 3 cups lemon juice
- 1 cup superfine sugar
- 1 large block ice
- 1/2 pint curaçao
- 1/2 pint brandy
- 3 quarts claret (red Bordeaux wine)
- 1 quart chilled club soda
- Fruits in season

### Direction

- Mix sugar together with lemon juice, stirring until the sugar dissolves. In a punch bowl, insert ice before pouring in the sweetened lemon juice. Stir and add the club soda, wine, brandy and curacao. Serve the drinks in punch glasses about 4-oz. in size and garnish with fruit.

## 29. Coconut-curry Sauce

*"Serve with sake marinated sea bass and coconut curry sauce, or if desired, with shrimps or chicken"*
*Serving: Makes about 2 cups*

### Ingredients

- 1/2 cup mirin*
- 1/4 cup chopped fresh lemongrass**
- 1 tbsp. chopped peeled fresh ginger
- 1/4 cup dry white wine
- 2 cups whipping cream
- 3/4 cup canned unsweetened coconut milk*
- 2 tsps. Thai green or red curry paste*
- *Available at Asian markets and in the Asian foods section of some supermarkets.
- **Fresh lemongrass can be found in the produce section (not Asian foods section) of some supermarkets.

### Direction

- Boil lemongrass, ginger and mirin in a heavy medium pot for six minutes or until it lessens to 1/4 cup. Add wine and continue boiling for another six minutes until it reduces to 1/4 cup. Add the coconut milk and the cream and boil on high heat. Reduce heat to medium and let simmer for 12 minutes, stirring occasionally. When the mixture is slightly thickened, stir in the curry paste and season to taste with pepper and salt. Keep aside to cool and refrigerate if you plan to use the next day. Before serving, warm on medium heat.

## 30. Coq Au Vin

*""During important celebrations, I always make this and I get praises every single time. The beautiful dish comprises burgundy wine, herbs and vegetables cooked with chicken. To complete the meal, simply add salad, bread or noodles.""*
*Serving: 4 | Prep: 20m | Ready in: 1h20m*

### Ingredients

- 4 skinless, boneless chicken breast halves
- 2 cups small whole fresh mushrooms
- 1 cup thinly sliced carrots
- 1 cup Burgundy wine
- 16 pearl onions, peeled
- 1 tbsp. bacon bits
- 1 tbsp. chopped fresh parsley
- 2 cloves garlic, minced
- 3/4 tsp. dried marjoram, crushed
- 3/4 tsp. dried thyme, crushed
- 1/2 tsp. chicken bouillon granules
- 1/8 tsp. ground black pepper
- 1 bay leaf
- 1 1/2 cups cold water
- 1/8 cup all-purpose flour

### Direction

- Use cooking spray to layer a big non-stick skillet then insert the chicken. Over moderate heat, sauté the chicken for around 15 minutes until both sides have browned slightly.
- Throw in the bay leaf, pepper, bouillon, thyme, marjoram, garlic, parsley, bacon bits, onions, wine, carrot and mushrooms and lead it to boil. Lower the heat and leave it simmering covered until the chicken becomes thoroughly cooked with no shade of pink left, about 25 minutes.
- Move the onions, carrot, mushrooms and chicken with a slotted spoon onto a platter, getting rid of the bay leaf. Cover the platter up to maintain warmth and put it to one side. Whisk water and flour together in a small bowl then pour it into the skillet. Stir for 5 to 10 minutes until it begins to bubble and

thicken into the skillet. For 1 minute, continue stirring and cooking. Pour the veggies and mixture over the chicken. Serve the dish warm.

## Nutrition Information

- Calories: 242 calories;
- Total Carbohydrate: 13.1 g
- Cholesterol: 70 mg
- Total Fat: 2.2 g
- Protein: 30.7 g
- Sodium: 210 mg

## 31. Coq Au Vin With Cocoa Powder

*"Coq au vin recipe featuring deliciously browned mushrooms and chicken with smooth sauce."*
*Serving: 4 servings*

## Ingredients

- 1 (3 1/2–4-lb.) chicken, cut into 8 pieces (legs and thighs separated, breasts halved)
- Kosher salt, freshly ground pepper
- 1 large yellow onion, chopped
- 1 large carrot, peeled, chopped
- 1 bunch thyme
- 2 bay leaves
- 1 (750 ml) bottle red wine, preferably Côte du Rhône
- 3 tbsps. olive oil, divided
- 2 tbsps. unsalted butter, divided
- 5 oz. thick-cut bacon, cut into 1/4-inch pieces
- 8 oz. button mushrooms, halved
- 1 tbsp. all-purpose flour
- 8 oz. pearl onions, peeled
- 1 tbsp. red wine vinegar
- 1 tbsp. unsweetened cocoa powder

## Direction

- Sprinkle pepper and salt all over chicken; put in a big bowl. Add wine, yellow onion, bay leaves, carrot, and thyme; cover. Refrigerate chicken for at least 1-2 days, flip 1-2 times.
- Take the chicken out of the marinade then use paper towels to pat dry. Do not throw away the marinade. Remove any herbs that stick to the chicken. Filter marinade on a sieve with a fine mesh into a big bowl. Separate aromatics and infused wine; set aside.
- On medium heat, heat a tbsp. each of butter and oil in a big Dutch oven or any heavy saucepan. Cook and stir frequently bacon for 5-8mins until crispy and brown. Move bacon on a medium bowl using a slotted spoon.
- In a single layer, put chicken in the same pot with its skin-side down and cook for 8-10mins until the skin is brown. Move chicken on a plate with its skin-side up.
- Leave three tbsps. of fat on the pot and turn to medium-high heat, keep other fat further use. Cook and stir mushrooms for 5mins until tender and brown, pour in infused wine once there are dark bits forming at the base of the pot. Move mushrooms in the bowl of bacon.
- Once the base of the pot is dry, ladle a tbsp. or more of reserved fat. Cook and stir frequently saved aromatics for 8-10mins until the veggies are soft and brown on the sides. Dust flour on top; cook and stir until there is no visible flour. In a single layer, place the chicken back with its skin-side up in the pot; add in saved infused wine. The liquid should be over the chicken, pour in water if necessary. Let it simmer while slightly covered. Cook for 30-40mins until an inserted thermometer on the meatiest breast part reads 160 degrees F.
- On medium heat, heat the remaining two tbsp. oil and a tbsp. butter in a medium pan. Put in pearl onions and a sprinkle of salt. Cook for 8-10mins while shaking the pan regularly until the onions are brown. Pour in enough water until the onions are just about covered then partially cover skillet with the lid; boil. Lower heat and let it simmer for 15-20mins until the onions are soft all the way through. Let it stand.
- Move chicken on a plate and cover with a sheet of foil. Using a sieve with a fine mesh,

filter braising liquid into a big bowl; remove the solids. Place the liquid back in the pot on medium heat. In a small bowl, stir three tbsps. braising liquid, cocoa, and vinegar together until smooth. Incorporate mixture into the pot with braising liquid and let it simmer. Cook and stir from time to time for 5-10mins until the sauce is silky smooth and a bit thick. Put in saved mushrooms, bacon and pearl onions including the cooking liquid. Cook until the mixture is warmed through. Place the chicken back in the pot.

## Nutrition Information

- Calories: 1141
- Total Carbohydrate: 21 g
- Cholesterol: 256 mg
- Total Fat: 74 g
- Fiber: 4 g
- Protein: 62 g
- Sodium: 1963 mg
- Saturated Fat: 22 g

## 32. Cornish Hen In Port Wine And Fig Preserves

*"For deeper colored ingredients, use port wine. To serve two people, use Cornish game hens. They are also the perfect size for the slow cooker. For the creation of a simple sauce for meats, go for jellies, jams and preserves."*
*Serving: Serves 2*

## Ingredients

- 1 Cornish game hen
- Salt
- Freshly ground black pepper
- 2 sprigs fresh rosemary
- 1/4 cup fig preserves
- 1/4 cup port wine

## Direction

- If desired, use a cooking spray to coat inside of a slow cooker sized 3-1/2 quart. Scatter a

generous amount of pepper and salt onto the hen. Put the rosemary into the cavity and put the hen into the slow cooker.

- In a small bowl, combine the port wine with fig preserves before dispensing it out into the slow cooker over the hen. Put the lid on and set the temperature to high. Cook the hen for 5 hours.
- Try it out then add pepper and salt to season to taste. Serve the hen with sauce over it.

## Nutrition Information

- Calories: 476
- Total Carbohydrate: 31 g
- Cholesterol: 170 mg
- Total Fat: 24 g
- Fiber: 1 g
- Protein: 29 g
- Sodium: 527 mg
- Saturated Fat: 7 g

## 33. Crab Cakes With Chardonnay Cream Sauce

*"Crushing the potato chips is the mystery behind the wonderful, crispy coating."*
*Serving: Serves 8 as a first-course*

## Ingredients

- 1 3/4 cups Chardonnay or other dry white wine
- 1/3 cup chopped shallots
- 1 cup whipping cream
- 1 1/2 lbs. crabmeat, drained (about 4 cups)
- 2 1/2 cups finely crushed potato chips
- 1 1/4 cups fresh breadcrumbs made from French bread
- 1 7.25-oz. jar roasted red peppers, drained, coarsely chopped
- 1/2 cup thinly sliced green onions
- 2 large eggs
- 2 tbsps. chopped fresh dill
- 1 tbsp. Dijon mustard
- 1 tbsp. whole grain mustard

- 1 tbsp. mayonnaise
- 1/4 cup (about) vegetable oil

## Direction

- In a heavy midsized saucepan, boil the shallots and wine for around 10 minutes until the mixture reduces to half a cup. For the next 10 minutes, boil the cream until the liquid is reduced into the consistency of sauce. Add pepper and salt to your liking.
- In a big bowl, combine the following 7 ingredients together with breadcrumbs, half cup of crushed potato chips and crabmeat until they are properly mixed together. For every cake, make use of 1/4 cupful of crab mixture to be shaped into sixteen cakes with 2-1/2 inch diameter each (This can be done 6 hours in advance. Seal the crab cakes and cover sauce independently and keep them in the fridge. Over medium low heat, heat and stir occasionally to rewarm sauce before serving).
- Insert the rest of the potato chips into a shallow dish. To coat the cake evenly, push each cake into the bowl of chips.
- In a big, heavy skillet, heat 2 tbsps. of oil over medium-high heat before adding the crab cakes in batch by batch. Cook each side for 5 minutes until thoroughly heated and golden brown in color. Pour in more oil if needed. Line a plate with paper towel before moving the cake crabs onto it in order to drain the oil off. Set 2 crab cakes per plate then ladle sauce surrounding the crab cakes. Serve immediately.

## Nutrition Information

- Calories: 429
- Total Carbohydrate: 26 g
- Cholesterol: 146 mg
- Total Fat: 26 g
- Fiber: 2 g
- Protein: 18 g
- Sodium: 681 mg
- Saturated Fat: 8 g

## 34. Cucumber Sake-tini

""*I warn you that this martini is totally deadly because the cooling cucumber masks the gin's potency. The mint raises the general floral bouquet and the sake adds a little "je ne sais quoi". We often serve this refreshing beverage at our Southern Supper Club due to popular demand.*""
*Serving: Makes about 2 1/2 cups/600 ml; serves 2*

## Ingredients

- 3/4 cup/180 ml gin
- 1/4 cup/60 ml premium sake
- 1/4 cup/60 ml fresh lime juice
- 2 cups/280 g peeled, seeded, and diced cucumber, frozen
- 1/2 cup/85 g green grapes, frozen
- 1/4 cup/10 g firmly packed fresh mint leaves
- 2 tbsp agave nectar
- Pinch of sea salt

## Direction

- Combine lime juice, agave nectar, salt, grapes, gin, mint, cucumber, and sake in a blender. Blend the mixture until smooth and frothy.

## Nutrition Information

- Calories: 382
- Total Carbohydrate: 33 g
- Total Fat: 0 g
- Fiber: 3 g
- Protein: 2 g
- Sodium: 67 mg
- Saturated Fat: 0 g

## 35. Damn The Weather II

*Serving: Makes 6 drinks*

## Ingredients

- 2 cups Ruby Port
- 1 cup unsweetened pineapple juice

- 1 cup fresh orange juice
- 1 tsp. fresh lemon juice
- Chilled club soda or seltzer water
- 6 lemon slices for garnish

## Direction

- Blend the juices and port together into a big pitcher. Prepare 6 glasses to fill with ice cubes. Distribute drink among glasses and pour soda on top. Add slices of lemon for garnishing.

---

## 36. Delicate Bread Pudding

*"Tasty puddings with silky custard on the bottom served with orange sauce."*
*Serving: Serves 6*

## Ingredients

- 25 oz. brioche, sliced
- 4 cups whole milk, at room temperature
- 3 large eggs, separated
- 1/2 cup sugar
- Pinch of salt
- 1 tsp. vanilla extract
- 1/2 cup sugar, or more to taste
- Grated zest and juice of 1 large orange, or more juice to taste
- 1 cup water
- 1/2 cup dry white wine or cherry or plum eau-de-vie

## Direction

- For the puddings, preheat oven to 350 degrees F and butter 6 ten-oz. ramekins. In a pot, mix milk and brioche together; set aside for 10mins.
- On medium-high heat, put the pot and cook until the milk bubbles on the edges. Take off heat.
- Beat sugar and egg yolks together in a bowl until pale and light using a hand mixer or in a mixer with the paddle attachment. Softly whisk the hot brioche mixture with the eggs.

Let it disintegrate to chunks without turning it to mash.

- In a big bowl or a mixer bowl, beat salt and egg whites until it forms into soft peaks; stir in vanilla. Mix the whites into the bread mix. Spoon the pudding on ramekins. Fill baking dish with enough boiling water, place the ramekins in the dish. Make sure that the water is halfway to the sides of the ramekins.
- Bake puddings for 25-35mins until an inserted cake tester comes out without residue. Take the puddings out of the water bath.
- Meanwhile, start making the sauce. In a small pot, mix water, sugar, orange juice, and orange zest together; boil. Continue cooking for 5mins. Take off heat and mix in white wine; taste. If desired, adjust sugar and orange juice.
- Turn puddings in shallow bowls and ladle sauce over and around each portion. Serve

## Nutrition Information

- Calories: 629
- Total Carbohydrate: 102 g
- Cholesterol: 170 mg
- Total Fat: 15 g
- Fiber: 3 g
- Protein: 20 g
- Sodium: 605 mg
- Saturated Fat: 6 g

---

## 37. Etuvee De Veau Au Vin Rouge

*"Sit back and enjoy the dish with a nice glass of wine."*
*Serving: Serves 6*

## Ingredients

- 4 lbs. leg of veal, boned and cut in 2" cubes
- 6 small onions, thinly sliced
- 6 tbsps. butter
- Flour seasoned with salt and pepper
- Red wine (Beaujolais)
- 7-8 shallots, finely chopped
- 3 cloves garlic, finely chopped
- 1 tbsp. fresh (or 1 tsp. dried) basil

- Garnish: finely chopped parsley

## Direction

- Sauté the onions with butter until just wilted then add meat cubes rolled in seasoned flour into the pan. Sauté the veal until browned on all sides then pour adequate red wine in to cover the basil, garlic and shallots. Cover and cook in an oven at 325°F until veal turns tender, about 2-1/2 to 3 hours. Move the meat to a hot platter and layer sauce over it (for a thicker sauce, return it to the top of the stove and mix it with beurre manié). Decorate with chopped parsley. Serve together with boiled new potatoes and cooked, chopped up spinach flavored with lemon juice, olive oil and garlic. Enjoy this dish with fine red Beaujolais.

---

## 38. Flounder With Corn And Tasso Maque Choux

*"The fish, cooked in foil, is best served with maque choux. Enjoy the rich flavor of herbs and citrus infused in the beer and wine."*
*Serving: Makes 4 servings*

## Ingredients

- 4 1/4-inch-thick shallot slices (rounds), divided
- 4 tbsps. (1/2 stick) unsalted butter, divided
- 4 small garlic cloves, sliced, divided
- 8 thin slices unpeeled lime, divided
- 4 thin slices unpeeled orange, divided
- 4 6- to 7-oz. flounder or John Dory fillets (preferably with skin)
- Cayenne pepper
- 8 fresh thyme sprigs, divided
- 8 tbsps. dark beer, divided
- 4 tbsps. dry white wine, divided
- Corn and Tasso Maque Choux

## Direction

- Line a big pie dish with foil, allowing the foil to hang over one side. Slice one shallot and

place the rings on the foil along with one clove sliced garlic, two slices of lime, and one slice of orange. Top with one tbsp. of butter. In a separate dish, season the fillet of fish on both sides with cayenne and salt. Place the fillet on the foil, with the skin side down. Sprinkle with two sprigs of thyme. Pour a generous tbsp. of wine and two tbsps. of beer around the fish. Fold the extra foil over the fish and seal well by sealing it on 3 sides then again to make it double sealed. Place the sealed fish on a baking sheet. Repeat process for the rest of the fillets and seasonings.
- Place the packets, sealed side up on the grill of a preheated barbecue and cook for ten minutes or done on high heat. The fish should feel slightly firm to touch. Serve hot with Tasso Maque Choux and Corn.

---

## 39. Fresh Goat Cheese, Roasted Beet, And Walnut Tart

*"A bit of the beet juice may run off and colour the goat cheese as well as custard during baking, giving the tart a sort of marbleized look. This tart – a combination of goat cheese salad, walnut and classic beet – is particularly great with greens dressed in brilliant vinaigrette. It also makes for a wonderful side dish for grilled lamb chops."*
*Serving: Makes one 10-inch tart; Serves 6 to 8*

## Ingredients

- 2 to 3 small beets
- 1 tbsp. olive oil
- Kosher salt and freshly ground black pepper
- 1 tbsp. unsalted butter
- 1 medium onion, thinly sliced
- 2 tbsps. dry white wine
- 1 recipe Hamersley's Bistro Tart Dough , shaped and blind-baked according to the directions
- 3 large eggs
- 3/4 cup heavy cream
- 4 oz. fresh goat cheese
- 1 cup chopped walnuts (about 4 oz.)
- 1 tbsp. walnut oil (optional)

- About 2 tbsps. chopped fresh parsley

## Direction

- Heat the oven to 350°F. After washing the beets, use a paper towel to dry them up. Set them down in a small ovenproof pan. Drip olive oil over the beets and sprinkle pepper and salt to season them then use aluminium foil to cover the pan. Bake the beets for 1 hour or until they are tender when pierced with a paring knife.
- Let the beets cool off before peeling them with a small knife and cutting them up into a medium dice (It is advisable to wear gloves for this step as beet juice can stain counters, towels most things including your hands so be careful).
- In a frying pan, heat the butter over medium heat. Insert the onion and add a few dashes of salt to season. Cook for 7 minutes until the onion turns slightly tender, stirring every now and then. Pour in the white wine then leave it to cook for another minute, scrape up browned bits stuck from the bottom of the pan.
- Heat the oven to 350°F. Mix the onion and beets together and move them into the blind-baked tart shell.
- Beat cream and eggs together and add pepper and salt to season. Carefully pour this mixture over the onion and beets, allowing the cream to seep into the beets evenly. Distribute a dot of goat cheese all over the top of tart. On a baking sheet, set the tart down and bake for around 20 minutes. Scatter chopped walnuts over the tart and if using, drip the walnut oil over the top. Put the tart back into the oven and bake for an extra 15 to 20 minutes until just set. Before serving, top the tart with chopped parsley and let it sit for at least 5 minutes.

## Nutrition Information

- Calories: 476
- Total Carbohydrate: 27 g
- Cholesterol: 148 mg
- Total Fat: 35 g
- Fiber: 4 g
- Protein: 14 g
- Sodium: 432 mg
- Saturated Fat: 13 g

## 40. Frosé (frozen Rosé) Ice Pops

*"If you're looking to celebrate the season of rosé and just beautiful sunny days, you should get some friends together to enjoy these boozy, fruity ice pops together."*
*Serving: Makes 10 | Prep: 15m*

## Ingredients

- 6 oz. strawberries, hulled (about 1 1/2 cups)
- 2 oz. fresh raspberries (about 1/3 cup)
- 1 2/3 cups dry rosé (about half of a 750 ml bottle)
- 1/2 cup ruby red grapefruit juice, preferably fresh
- 2 tbsps. sugar
- 1 cup whole or sliced fresh strawberries and raspberries
- 10 (2.5-oz.) freezer ice-pop molds and sticks

## Direction

- In a blender, puree the grapefruit juice, rosé, raspberries, sugar and strawberries on a high speed until smooth. Using a fine-mesh sieve, strain the mixture into a big measuring cup then get rid of the foam and seeds. Distribute the strawberry mixture equally into ice-pop moulds and keep the top one-inch unoccupied. Freeze it for an hour until it turns slushy then stir it using the ice-pop stick. Insert fresh berries and incorporate them by stirring with the stick. Cover the moulds up, place the sticks in and let it freeze for a minimum of 4 hours or until the ice pops turn solidified. One can prepare the ice pops three months in advance. Simply freeze them until they're solid and keep them frozen inside of an airtight container.

## Nutrition Information

- Calories: 108
- Total Carbohydrate: 22 g
- Total Fat: 0 g
- Fiber: 2 g
- Protein: 0 g
- Sodium: 11 mg
- Saturated Fat: 0 g

## 41. Garlicky Linguine With Crab, Red Bell Pepper And Pine Nuts

*"Serving Parmesan with seafood pasta is an unusual thing but it works in this case. The cheese brings a lovely lushness to this pasta dish."*
*Serving: Makes 6 first-course or 4 main-course servings*

### Ingredients

- 5 tbsps. unsalted butter
- 1 red bell pepper, finely chopped
- 4 garlic cloves, finely chopped
- 1/4 tsp. dried crushed red pepper
- 1/2 cup dry white wine
- 12 oz. linguine
- 1 8-oz. bottle clam juice
- 1 lb. fresh lump crabmeat, picked over
- 1/4 cup finely chopped fresh parsley
- 1/3 cup pine nuts, toasted
- Freshly grated Parmesan cheese

### Direction

- In a big, sturdy skillet, melt butter over medium heat then add the bell pepper. Cover it up and cook for 2 minutes before adding the crushed red pepper and garlic. Cover it up and continue cooking for 2 minutes. Turn the heat up to high, pour the wine in and boil for 2 minutes before setting it aside.
- In a big pot of salted boiling water, cook and stir pasta until firm to the bite but just tender. Stir occasionally. Drain the pasta, reserving half a cup of the cooking water. Transfer the pasta back into the pot then add the bell pepper mixture, 1/2 cup of cooking water and clam juice. Over high heat, cook for 2 minutes until pasta absorbs half of the liquid then mix the crab in. Toss for 1 minute until thoroughly heated then add parsley, followed by pepper to season to taste. Distribute the pasta equally among bowls and sprinkle pine nuts. Offer the cheese in a separate bowl. Serve.

## Nutrition Information

- Calories: 439
- Total Carbohydrate: 46 g
- Cholesterol: 99 mg
- Total Fat: 16 g
- Fiber: 3 g
- Protein: 25 g
- Sodium: 686 mg
- Saturated Fat: 7 g

## 42. Gingerbread Trifle With Candied Kumquats And Wine-poached Cranberries

*"This recipe calls for two trifle dishes with diameter 7 3/4" and with a depth of 4 3/4". To assemble and serve, use a pretty looking glass. Cut four rounds from each cake layer, alternating two rounds with two or three layers of mascarpone cream, some poached cranberries and some candied kumquats."*
*Serving: Makes 12-16 servings*

### Ingredients

- 2 1/2 cups sugar
- 1 1/2 cups water
- 3 cups sliced seeded kumquats
- 2 cups fruity red wine (such as Syrah)
- 2 cups sugar
- 12 oz. fresh or frozen cranberries
- 1 cup extra stout (such as Guinness)
- 1 cup mild-flavored (light) molasses
- 1 1/2 tsps. baking soda
- 2 cups all purpose flour
- 2 tbsps. ground ginger

- 1 1/2 tsps. baking powder
- 3/4 tsp. ground cinnamon
- 1/4 tsp. ground cloves
- 1/4 tsp. ground nutmeg
- 1/8 tsp. ground cardamom
- 3 large eggs
- 1/2 cup sugar
- 1/2 cup (packed) dark brown sugar
- 3/4 cup vegetable oil
- 1 tbsp. minced peeled fresh ginger
- 3 8-oz. containers mascarpone cheese* (3 cups)
- 3 cups chilled heavy whipping cream
- 1 1/2 cups powdered sugar
- 3 tbsps. Grand Marnier or other orange liqueur
- 4 tsps. finely grated orange peel

## Direction

- To prepare the kumquats, heat 1 1/2 cups water in a big pan on medium heat. Stir in the sugar until it dissolves, then increase heat. Allow liquid starts boiling, add the kumquats. Reduce heat and allow to simmer on medium low. Transfer to a bowl, cover and refrigerated until cold. You can make these candied kumquats five days ahead of using. Store in refrigerator.
- When ready to use, drain syrup from the kumquats and reserve. Keep the kumquats aside for using in the trifle.
- To prepare the cranberries, dissolve sugar in wine in a big pan on medium heat. Increase heat and allow to boil for five minutes. Add the cranberries and allow to simmer for five minutes until they are soft, yet intact. Turn into a medium bowl and allow to cool. Cover and refrigerate until cold. You can make the wine poached cranberries five days ahead of using. Keep them chilled until ready to use.
- When ready to use, drain syrup from the cranberries and reserve. Keep the cranberries aside for using in the trifle.
- To make the gingerbread cake, place a big saucepan on medium high heat with the molasses and stout. Boil, stirring occasionally. Turn off the heat and stir in the baking soda.

When the soda is added, the mixture will start foaming; this is natural. Allow to cool for about an hour.

- Preheat oven to 350-degree F and place two racks, one in the top third and the second in the bottom third of the oven. Take three 8" cake pans having 1 1/2" high sides. Grease each generously with butter, and dust with flour. Turn pans over and tap out the excess flour. In a big bowl, whisk together two cups flour with the following six ingredients, until well blended. In another bowl whisk the eggs with both the sugars. When well blended, whisk in the oil followed by the stout mixture. Gradually whisk this into the flour mixture. Gently stir in the fresh ginger. Equally divide the batter into the prepared pans.
- Place the pans in the preheated oven; two on the top rack and the third on the bottom rack. Bake until done. Test by inserting a tester in the middle of the cakes. The tester should exit clean. Halfway through the baking, reverse the position of the pans. After around 28 minutes, when the cakes are done, remove from oven and cool on rack for 15 minutes. Invert the cakes on to the racks and allow to cool through. These cakes may be made one day ahead, wrapped in plastic and stored at room temperature.
- To make the mascarpone cheese, beat the mascarpone in a big bowl with an electric mixer. When the mixture is smooth, add the rest of the ingredients and continue beating until peaks form. Be careful not to overbeat as this will cause the mixture to curdle). Cover and refrigerate for a maximum of two hours.
- Cut each cake in half horizontally using a serrated knife. You will get four layers of cake. Trim one layer to a 7" round. Place this in the bottom of the trifle dish. Scatter 1/2 cup kumquats over the cake, in a single layer and spread 1 1/3 cups of the mascarpone cream evenly over the kumquats until the sides of the dish. Repeat with 1/2 cup cranberries. Place a cake layer over this and repeat the procedure until all the cake layers are used up. Transfer the remaining cream into a pastry bag and fit

it with a large star nozzle. Pipe pretty rosettes around the top edge of the dish. Cover the dish loosely with a large piece of foil and chill in the refrigerator for a minimum of four hours. You can make this dish one day ahead of serving. Cover and chill the remaining candied fruit.

- Before serving, scatter the top of the trifle with the leftover candied cranberries and kumquats.

## Nutrition Information

- Calories: 1243
- Total Carbohydrate: 143 g
- Cholesterol: 248 mg
- Total Fat: 72 g
- Fiber: 5 g
- Protein: 11 g
- Sodium: 423 mg
- Saturated Fat: 35 g

## 43. Glögg

*"A hearty, fun little Scandinavian Christmas Punch."*
*Serving: Serves 6*

## Ingredients

- 1 lemon
- 1 navel orange
- 1 (750-ml) bottle dry red wine
- 1/2 cup sugar
- 3 whole cloves
- 1 (1-inch) cinnamon stick
- 1/4 tsp. allspice
- 1 green cardamom pod
- 1 thin slice fresh ginger
- 1/2 cup Tawny Port
- 1/2 cup aquavit
- 1/4 cup kirsch
- 1/4 cup vodka
- 1/2 to 1 cup raisins (to taste)
- 1/3 cup blanched sliced almonds

## Direction

- Use a vegetable peeler to get the zest from orange and lemon, reserving the fruit for a different time. Over moderate heat, combine the ginger, spices, zests, sugar and half a bottle of red wine in a 2-quart saucepan. Stir until sugar dissolves and the just barely simmering and do not boil. Leave it on a gentle simmer for 10 minutes then let it cool down. Use a fine sieve to pour the mixture into a bowl. Pour the other alcohols and the remaining wine. In a clean saucepan over moderate heat, heat the mixture until just warm. Distribute almonds and raisins in between 6 heatproof glasses or small coffee cups before ladling in the glögg. Prepare little spoons to be served together for eating almonds and raisins.

## Nutrition Information

- Calories: 386
- Total Carbohydrate: 41 g
- Total Fat: 4 g
- Fiber: 3 g
- Protein: 3 g
- Sodium: 9 mg
- Saturated Fat: 0 g

## 44. Grilled Peaches With Vin Santo And Anise Biscotti

*"Serve this lip-smacking desert with a glass of sweet Italian white wine like Vin Santo."*
*Serving: Makes 4 servings*

## Ingredients

- 1/2 cup sugar
- 1/2 vanilla bean, split lengthwise
- 1 8-oz. container mascarpone cheese*
- 4 large firm but ripe peaches, halved, pitted
- 1 tbsp. safflower oil or vegetable oil
- 1 1/4 cups Vin Santo
- 1 1/2 tbsps. chilled unsalted butter
- Anise Biscottiepi:recipelink</epi:recipelink>

## Direction

- In a bowl, place the sugar and scrap in the seeds from the vanilla bean. Stir. In another bowl, combine mascarpone cheese with two tbsps. of vanilla sugar. This mixture can be made in advance and stored for up to one month at room temperature in an airtight container. Or it can be refrigerated, covered, for two days.
- Heat oven to 400-degree F and prepare the barbecue at medium heat. Cut peaches into halves and brush the cut sides lightly with oil. Place peach halves on a rack and grill, cut side down. When grill marks appear on the fruit, remove and place them in a medium sized baking dish, cut sides up.
- Boil Vin Santo in a small pan. Gently pour 1/2 cup of the heated Vin Santo over the fruit and sprinkle with three tbsps. of vanilla sugar. Bake for 15 minutes until the peaches are tender. Boil and reduce and leftover 3/4 cup Vin Santo for 4 minutes until it reduces to three tbsps.. Stir in butter until it melts.
- Transfer each peach half onto individual serving plates. Place a good dollop of mascarpone alongside the fruit. Drizzle with the heated Vin Santo and serve warm. This dish can also be served at room temperature. Serve with Anise.

---

## 45. Herb-crusted Beef Rib Roast With Potatoes, Carrots, And Pinot Noir Jus

*"Mesmerize your guests this Christmas season with this delicious beef rib roast. Serve it with sauce."*
*Serving: Makes 10 servings | Prep: 1h*

## Ingredients

- 1 (4-rib) standing beef rib roast (bone-in prime rib; 9 to 10 lbs.)
- 1/4 cup mixed peppercorns (pink, white, and green)
- 3 tbsps. plus 2 1/2 tsps. kosher salt, divided
- 2 tbsps. chopped fresh thyme
- 2 tbsps. chopped fresh rosemary
- 1 tbsp. extra-virgin olive oil
- 3 lbs. medium Yukon Gold potatoes, peeled and each cut into 6 wedges (keep in a bowl of cold water to prevent discoloration)
- 3 lbs. carrots, peeled and cut diagonally into 2-inch pieces
- 1 (750 milliliter) bottle Pinot Noir
- 1/2 cup chopped shallots
- 4 tbsps. unsalted butter, divided
- 2 1/4 cups reduced-salt beef or chicken broth
- Heavy flameproof roasting pan (not glass) fitted with a flat rack; instant-read thermometer; 2 (18- by 13-inch) heavy rimmed sheet pans (aka half-sheet pans); parchment paper

## Direction

- Arrange the roast, fat side up, on a rack in a roasting pan after patting it dry.
- Coarsely crush and combine peppercorns in a small bowl then mix with thyme, 3 tbsps. kosher salt and rosemary inside a small bowl.
- Place roast on a baking tray and rub oil all over it. Sprinkle the peppercorn mixture and press with fingers so it sticks to the roast. Let stand for one hour, at room temperature.
- Place roast on lowermost rack in preheated oven (450 deg F) and allow to roast for 20 minutes.
- Reduce temperature to 350-degree F and continue to roast for approximately two hours or until an instant read thermometer reads 110-degree F when inserted in the middle of the roast. Transfer the roast onto a clean platter and let it stand for 40 minutes without covering it. Retain the fat and pan juice in the pan.
- Increase the temperature of the oven to 450-degree F and place another rack in the uppermost position in the oven. Line another baking sheet with parchment paper.
- In a glass measuring jug, carefully strain the reserved pan juices. Toss well drained potatoes in a big bowl, along with 1 tsp.

kosher salt and 3 tbsps. of the strained liquid. Spread out the marinated potatoes on the lined baking sheet. In the same bowl, throw in and toss carrots with the same quantity of kosher salt and strained liquid. Spread the carrots out on another baking tray. Place the trays, one in the uppermost part of the oven and the other in the lowermost part. Stir occasionally and switch the trays a couple of times halfway through the roasting process. Toast for about 30 minutes or until the vegetables are golden. The potatoes may take a few minutes longer.

- While the vegetables are in the oven, prepare the jus. Skim the fat from the strained juice and discard. Place the pan on two burners and add one cup wine and allow to boil on high heat, to deglaze the pan. Scrape up any brown bits. Pour the liquid into a cup.
- In a big and heavy three- or four-quart saucepan, lightly heat one tbsp. butter. Season with 1/4 tsp. kosher salt and sauté shallots, over medium heat, for just under five minutes or until golden brown. Add the prepared wine mixture and the leftover wine. Boil on high heat for approximately ten minutes until the liquid reduces to 3/4 cup.
- Add broth to the mixture in the pan while it is on high heat and continue to boil until the liquid reduces to 1 1/2 cups. Strain liquid into a separate saucepan and drop in the diced 3 tbsps. butter. Whisk well and season with pepper and salt.
- Carve roast to separate the meat from the bones and slice meat. Serve with the prepared jus and vegetables.

## Nutrition Information

- Calories: 1038
- Total Carbohydrate: 44 g
- Cholesterol: 175 mg
- Total Fat: 70 g
- Fiber: 8 g
- Protein: 43 g
- Sodium: 1504 mg
- Saturated Fat: 29 g

## 46. Honey-dew And Sake Granita

*"This fruity dessert with a wine twist is simple and quick to make."*
*Serving: Serves 4*

### Ingredients

- 1/2 cup sugar
- the flesh of a 3-lb. honeydew melon plus, if desired, 8 thin round slices of honeydew melon for garnish
- 1/4 cup sake
- 2 tsps. fresh lime juice
- 2/3 cup sugar
- 2 tbsps. pickled ginger slices (available at Asian markets and some supermarkets), rinsed
- 1/4 cup plum wine
- 2 drops of red food coloring if desired

### Direction

- Combine 3-1/2 cups of water and sugar together in a small saucepan and bring it to a boil, stirring throughout. Puree the syrup, food coloring, wine and ginger in a blender and leave the mixture to chill until it turns cold. Stir it. Move this mixture into a shallow metal pan or a 2-metal ice cube tray without the dividers and freeze it until it turns firm but is not frozen solid yet, about 2 to 3 hours. Every half an hour during this process, stir and crush the lumps with a fork. The granita can be prepared 2 days ahead of time and stored in a frozen state with a cover on. Use a fork to scrape the granita gently to soften the texture. Prepare 4 plates. On each one, set down two slices of honeydew and layer one of the pieces with sake granita and a scoop of honeydew then top other slices with plum-wine granita and a scoop of pickled ginger.

## 47. Hot Sangria

*"We absolutely adore this fruity wine mixture. It's very calming and soothing."*
*Serving: Makes 4 drinks.*

### Ingredients

- 1/4 cup sugar
- 1/2 cup fresh orange juice
- 1 bottle dry red wine
- 1/4 cup orange-flavored liqueur
- 4 lemon slices
- 4 orange slices, 1 slice stuck with 4 cloves

### Direction

- Mix 1/2 cup of water, juice and sugar together in a saucepan. For 5 minutes, stir and simmer the mixture. Whisk in the orange slices, lemon slices, liqueur and wine and heat it up at medium heat. Stir throughout until the mixture turns hot. Remove the orange slices and lemon slices and throw them away. Get 4 mugs that are already heated and distribute the mixture equally amongst them.

### Nutrition Information

- Calories: 306
- Total Carbohydrate: 37 g
- Total Fat: 0 g
- Fiber: 2 g
- Protein: 1 g
- Sodium: 10 mg
- Saturated Fat: 0 g

## 48. Instant Pot Sticky Hoisin Baby Back Ribs

*"These pressure-cooked ribs are tender without the meat shredding."*
*Serving: 4 main course or 8 appetizer servings | Prep: 25m*

### Ingredients

- 4 lb. baby back pork ribs (about 2 racks)
- 2 tsp. kosher salt
- 1 tsp. freshly ground black pepper
- 1/3 cup hoisin sauce
- 1/3 cup honey
- 1/3 cup soy sauce, preferably dark
- 2 Tbsp. Shaoxing rice wine or dry sherry
- 1 Tbsp. finely chopped fresh ginger
- 1/2 tsp. five-spice powder
- Flaky sea salt
- An Instant Pot

### Direction

- Turn meat into separate ribs by slicing in between the bones; sprinkle pepper and kosher salt. Set aside for at least half to full hour at room temperature.
- In a cooker insert, combine five-spice powder, hoisin, ginger, honey, rice wine, and soy sauce. Coat ribs in sauce and arrange in a single layer while fitting as many as possible; put the left ribs on the surface. Secure lid and position the steam release valve properly sealed. Turn the cooker in "Manual" and set to high pressure for 12mins.
- Once done, turn the cooker off. Use "Quick Release" to let out the steam then remove the lid. A sharp knife should easily go through the tender meat. Move meat on a platter.
- Set the cooker on "Sauté" mode and simmer the cooking liquid for 10-15mins until it reduces by 1/2.
- Preheat broiler or set the charcoal/gas grill on medium direct heat. Slather sauce over ribs. On direct heat, arrange ribs on the grate with their meat-side down. Grill for 5mins, covered, until crisp and brown in places or put on a

baking dish with their meat-side up then broil in the same manner.

- Place ribs in a platter then sprinkle sea salt. Serve ribs with leftover sauce.
- For a more fruity sauce, use orange or pineapple juice instead of honey. Instead of 5-spice powder, you can also use a pinch of crushed red pepper flakes or cayenne.

## Nutrition Information

- Calories: 1357
- Total Carbohydrate: 35 g
- Cholesterol: 370 mg
- Total Fat: 88 g
- Fiber: 1 g
- Protein: 105 g
- Sodium: 1979 mg
- Saturated Fat: 31 g

## 49.Jacques's French Potato Salad

*Serving: About 6 cups, serving 4 to 6*

## Ingredients

- 2 lbs. fingerling potatoes or other small waxy potatoes
- 1/2 cup or so extra-virgin olive oil
- 1/2 cup 1/4-inch slices of scallion, green and white parts
- 1/2 cup chopped onion
- 3 cloves garlic, mashed and coarsely chopped (1 1/2 tsp)
- 1/3 cup white wine
- 1 1/2 tbsps. Dijon-style mustard
- 2 to 3 tbsps. chopped chives
- 2 tbsps. or more coarsely chopped fresh green or purple basil, fresh tarragon, or parsley
- 1 tsp. kosher salt, plus more if needed
- 1/2 tsp. freshly cracked black pepper (coarse), plus more if needed
- Large radicchio leaves, about 6, from the outside of the head
- 1 or 2 hard-boiled eggs, coarsely chopped
- Chopped fresh parsley

## Direction

- Scrub the potatoes and put them whole in a saucepan. Cover them with water, about 1/2-inch. Let the water boil. Lower the heat and cook the potatoes until they can be pierced by a sharp knife and tender. Drain immediately. Allow the potatoes to cool slightly. (As soon as the potatoes are cool enough to handle, you can scrape the skin from the cooked potatoes. Scrape off only a band of skin, about 1/2-inch thick, all around the long ends of the potato for a decorative display with fingerlings.)
- In a small sauté pan, heat 2 tbsp. of olive oil. When the oil is already hot, add the onion and scallions, tossing well to coat. Let it cook for a minute over medium-high heat. Add garlic and toss well. Cook for a few minutes before removing the pan from the heat.
- While still warm, slice the potatoes crosswise into 1/2-inch sections. Place the slices in a large mixing bowl. Pour in the wine and 3-4 tbsp. of olive oil over them. Toss the mixture well to combine. Add the warm vegetables from the pan together with the chopped herbs, pepper, chives, mustard, and salt. Gently fold and combine them together, careful not to crush the potatoes. Season the salad according to your taste.
- Serve the potatoes warm (or at room temperature, and not colder). If you want, arrange the large radicchio leaves in a close circle on the serving platter, curved insides up until it forms a rough bowl. Spoon the potato salad inside the leaves. Sprinkle the edges with chopped egg. Top with parsley.

## Nutrition Information

- Calories: 318
- Total Carbohydrate: 10 g
- Cholesterol: 56 mg
- Total Fat: 29 g
- Fiber: 2 g
- Protein: 4 g
- Sodium: 361 mg
- Saturated Fat: 4 g

## 50. Jellied Apple Cranberry Sauce

*Serving: Serves 8*

### Ingredients

- a 12-oz. bag of cranberries, picked over
- 2 large Granny Smith apples (about 1 lb.)
- 1 cup dry white wine
- 1 1/2 cups sugar
- mint sprigs for garnish

### Direction

- Mix coarsely chopped apples (not cored or skinned), sugar, wine, and cranberries together in a bit pot; boil and stir. Let it simmer, covered, for 15mins while stirring from time to time. For another 20-25mins, let the mixture simmer without cover until it reduces to three cups of thick mixture. Press the mixture in a bowl through a food mill with a fine disk attachment. Scoop the mixture into a greased 3-4cup mold; refrigerate while covered overnight. Using a thin knife, run around the sides of the mold. Submerge the mold for 10secs on warm water. Turn the mold on a serving dish. Add mint sprigs and cranberry sauce on top.

### Nutrition Information

- Calories: 209
- Total Carbohydrate: 50 g
- Total Fat: 0 g
- Fiber: 3 g
- Protein: 0 g
- Sodium: 3 mg
- Saturated Fat: 0 g

## 51. Lamb En Daube

*Serving: Serves 6*

### Ingredients

- Shoulder of lamb, boned, larded, and cut in thick slices
- Salt, freshly ground black pepper, thyme, basil
- 1 small onion, finely chopped
- 1 carrot, finely chopped
- 4 cloves garlic, finely chopped
- Red wine
- 2 medium onions, chopped
- 8 slices bacon or salt pork, chopped
- 1/2 cup chopped parsley
- Orange rind
- Slices of larding pork

### Direction

- Combine the lamb chops, 1 tsp. pepper, small slices of onion, 2 finely sliced cloves of garlic, 1 tsp. salt, 1 tsp. thyme, carrot, 1 tsp. of basil, and red wine, enough to cover lamb chops in a deep pan. Set aside to marinate, 2 hours.
- Prepare a terrine or casserole and put one half of lamb slice at the bottom. Use the right size casserole to fit the meat tightly together. Place a layer of sliced onion, salt pork or bacon, the rest of the garlic combined with a few thymes, parsley, and basil incorporated all together. Sprinkle a few pieces of the orange rind. Put the remaining meat into the casserole, arrange it tightly over the layer of seasoning. Add marinade by straining over the casserole, enough to barely cover the layer of meat. Add larding pork strips over; cover. Set oven to 325 degrees F and cook casserole for 2 hours, covered. Lower heat to 300 degrees and bake for an additional 1 1/2 hours. Lastly, lower heat to 275 degrees F and bake, 1 hour. Serve while hot or cold with a crispy green salad and boiled potatoes. Perfect also with Château Cos d'Estournal red wine.

## 52. Lemon Zabaglione

*Serving: Makes about 6 cups*

### Ingredients

- 2 large eggs
- 4 large egg yolks
- 1/2 cup sugar
- Grated zest of 2 lemons
- Juice of 1 lemon
- 1/3 cup Muscat or other dessert wine

### Direction

- Prepare a double boiler. Take a saucepan and fill with 2" water. Lower a stainless steel bowl into the saucepan and place all the ingredients in it. Bring the water to a simmer.
- Whisk egg mixture in bowl vigorously until it becomes frothy and thick, and triples in quantity. Carefully lift the steel bowl off the saucepan a couple of times to release the steam. This will ensure the mixture does not start setting. After eight minutes take the bowl off the heat and continue to whisk lightly until cooled. Serve immediately. The mixture can be covered and stored for up to two hours. Whisk lightly before serving.

### Nutrition Information

- Calories: 142
- Total Carbohydrate: 21 g
- Cholesterol: 185 mg
- Total Fat: 5 g
- Fiber: 1 g
- Protein: 4 g
- Sodium: 30 mg
- Saturated Fat: 2 g

## 53. Lillet Au Citron

*"A refreshing lemon syrup and Lillet cocktail."*
*Serving: Makes 2 drinks.*

### Ingredients

- 1/4 cup sugar
- 1/4 cup fresh lemon juice
- ice cubes if desired
- 1 cup white Lillet
- chilled soda water
- 2 lemon slices for garnish if desired

### Direction

- Boil lemon juice and sugar in a small pot; stir until the sugar dissolves. Let it simmer for five minutes; cool completely. Put ice in two glasses; combine 1-2tbsp of lemon syrup to taste and half cup of Lillet in each glass. Pour in soda water and add lemon slices on top.

## 54. Mamaleh's Brisket

*"Use the fattier portion of the brisket, or the point cut for this delicious and tender dish."*
*Serving: 8 servings*

### Ingredients

- 1 (6–8-lb.) piece untrimmed point- or flat-cut beef brisket
- 1 tbsp. freshly ground black pepper
- 1/4 cup Diamond Crystal or 2 tbsps. plus 2 tsps. Morton kosher salt; plus more
- 1/4 cup schmaltz (chicken fat) or vegetable oil
- 2 large onions, coarsely chopped
- 5 large carrots, peeled, coarsely chopped
- 5 celery stalks, coarsely chopped
- 1 1/2 cups Manischewitz Concord grape wine or Concord grape juice
- 2 heads of garlic, halved crosswise
- 8 sprigs thyme
- 4 fresh bay leaves
- 2 tbsps. black peppercorns
- 3 quarts low-sodium chicken broth

## Direction

- Rub 2tbsp and 2tsp Morton salt or quarter cup Diamond crystal and ground pepper all over and into the grain of the brisket. Use a plastic wrap to tightly envelop the brisket; refrigerate for at least three hours to three days.
- Arrange the rack on the bottom third of the oven; preheat to 275 degrees F. In a big roasting pan, heat schmaltz on two burners set on high. Remove the brisket wrap. Cook for 7-10mins on each side until brown, lower heat if necessary; move on a baking sheet.
- Turn to medium-high heat; put in celery, carrots, onions, and salt. Cook for 15-18mins until soft and brown, stir from time to time. Pour in wine then boil; cook for 8-10mins until the wine evaporates. Put in broth, garlic, peppercorns, thyme, and bay leaves; boil. Place the brisket on top of the herbs and use a foil to cover firmly. Braise brisket for 2-3hrs until the meat is tender while still maintaining its shape. Allow the brisket to cool then refrigerate for 8hrs to two days.
- Preheat the oven to 250 degrees F. Skim and discard the fat on top of the braising liquid. Move brisket on a dish. Sieve the braising mixture on a big measuring glass to remove the solids. Pour the liquid back into the pan. On medium high heat, cook for half an hour until the liquid is smooth, flavorful but not salty, and has reduced by 1/2. Stir the liquid from time to time.
- Place the brisket back in the pan; use a sheet of foil to cover. Warm in the oven for 1 to 1 1/2 hrs. Move on a cutting board and cut the meat against its grain. Place the sliced meat on a dish and pour on braising liquid.

## Nutrition Information

- Calories: 1308
- Total Carbohydrate: 26 g
- Cholesterol: 373 mg
- Total Fat: 98 g
- Fiber: 4 g
- Protein: 80 g
- Sodium: 1358 mg

- Saturated Fat: 37 g

## 55. Manhattan Cooler II

*Serving: Serves 1*

## Ingredients

- 1 navel orange
- 2 jiggers (3 oz.) dry red wine
- 1 pony (1 oz.) dark rum
- 2 tsps. superfine granulated sugar
- 1/3 to 2/3 cup chilled seltzer

## Direction

- Starting at the navel end and working around the orange, remove the rind with a lemon zester to create an unbroken spiral string.
- Mix sugar, wine, and rum in a tall glass until the sugar is dissolved. Arrange the orange spiral into the glass, hooking one end of it over the edge. Fill it with ice. Add the seltzer.

## Nutrition Information

- Calories: 270
- Total Carbohydrate: 28 g
- Total Fat: 0 g
- Fiber: 3 g
- Protein: 1 g
- Sodium: 30 mg
- Saturated Fat: 0 g

## 56. Marinated Leg Of Lamb

*Serving: Serves 6*

## Ingredients

- 1 good-size leg spring lamb, boned and tied
- rosemary or tarragon
- 2 to 3 onions, thinly sliced
- 1 bay leaf
- Few sprigs parsley

- 1 clove garlic
- 1 tsp. salt
- 1/2 tsp. freshly ground black pepper
- Red wine

## Direction

- Debone the leg, keeping the shank bone, and tie and meat firmly. Cut slits on surface of meat and push in slivered garlic. Rub well with tarragon and rosemary. Place the meat in a deep kettle along with bay leaf, onion, parsley, garlic, 1 tsp. rosemary, salt and pepper, and enough red wine to cover the meat halfway. Allow to stand in refrigerator for about two days, turning meat at regular intervals so that it is properly marinated.
- When ready to cook, remove from refrigerator and roast at 375-degree F, basting with the marinade at regular intervals. The rule to follow for every lb. of rare lamb is 15 minutes and 18 minutes for medium rare. The meat is cooked rare when a meat thermometer shows a reading of 140-degree F.
- Serve lamb with boiled white beans with chopped parsley and garlic, and olive oil and a glass of California Pinot Noir.

## 57. Marsala And Dried-fig Crostata

*"What a heart-warming and delicious tart, especially with ice cream. Yum!"*
*Serving: Makes 8 servings*

## Ingredients

- 1 1/4 lbs. dried Calimyrna figs, stemmed, coarsely chopped
- 1 3/4 cups dry Marsala
- 1 3/4 cups water
- 1/4 cup (packed) golden brown sugar
- 2 cinnamon sticks
- 1/8 tsp. ground cloves
- 2 1/4 cups all purpose flour
- 1/2 cup sugar
- 2 tsps. fennel seeds

- 1/4 tsp. salt
- 1/2 cup plus 6 tbsps. (1 3/4 sticks) unsalted butter, room temperature
- 2 large eggs
- Vanilla ice cream

## Direction

- Filling: In a big sturdy saucepan over high heat, mix all the ingredients together and bring it to a boil. Adjust the heat to moderately low and cover it up. Let it simmer for 1 hour until the figs turn very tender. Remove the cover and let it simmer for another 8 minutes until the liquid reduces a little. Pour the mixture into a midsized bowl and let it cool down slightly before putting it into the fridge. Leave it in the refrigerator for 45 minutes until it turns cool and thick, stirring it from time to time. Get rid of the cinnamon sticks. The filling can be done one day in advance, just keep it covered up and chilled.
- Crust: Preheat the oven to 375°F. In a processor, mix salt, fennel seeds, sugar and flour followed by 1 egg and butter. Process it with the on and off turns until dough forms. Shape the dough up into a ball and divide it into half. Press each half down until it's a flat disk. Roll 1 disk up in plastic wrap and refrigerate until it turns cold. Keep it in the fridge for a minimum of 30 minutes up to 1 day. Get a 10-inch diameter tart pan with removable bottom and press the rest of the dough up the sides and onto the bottom of the pan. Use a fork to pierce all over the bottom and leave it to chill for 10 minutes until firm. This can be prepped one day in advance, just keep it chilled and covered up.
- On a waxed paper, roll out the chilled dough disk into a 12-inch round shape then move the dough onto a baking sheet, on waxed paper without rim. Slice the dough up into twelve strips with 3/4-inch width and let them chill while filling tart. Distribute the filling equally into crust then put 6 dough strips over the top of the filling. Make sure the strips are spaced out evenly. Set the remaining 6 strips atop the initial 6 strips diagonally, creating a diamond

lattice pattern upon completion. Trim the strips by pressing the ends of them against the pan's edges. In a small bowl, whisk the remaining egg until blended then brush it over the lattice. Bake the tart for 55 minutes. It is done when the crust turns a deep golden and the juices are bubbling heavily around the edges. Let it cool on the rack for 1 hour before running a small knife through the sides of the pan to gently loosen the tart. Get rid of the sides. It can be enjoyed at room temperature or even a little warmed up. Serve together with ice cream.

## Nutrition Information

- Calories: 489
- Total Carbohydrate: 63 g
- Cholesterol: 100 mg
- Total Fat: 22 g
- Fiber: 4 g
- Protein: 6 g
- Sodium: 101 mg
- Saturated Fat: 13 g

## 58. Miso-glazed Black Cod On Sunflower Sprouts

*"Rich in protein and vitamin B, miso comes in two varieties. Shiro miso, which is white miso and, the darker miso pastes. The Japanese use a lot of mirin in their cuisine, and this is made from glutinous rice. You can get both these items at most Asian supermarkets."*
*Serving: Makes 4 servings | Prep: 15m*

## Ingredients

- 1/3 cup white miso (fermented soybean paste)
- 1/4 cup plus 1 tsp. mirin (sweet Japanese rice wine)
- 3 tbsps. unseasoned rice vinegar, divided
- 2 tbsps. minced peeled fresh ginger
- 4 tsps. toasted sesame oil (such as Asian), divided
- 4 6-oz. skinless black cod fillets
- 1/2 cup chopped green onions, divided

- 5 oz. sunflower sprouts

## Direction

- Combine 2 tbsps. vinegar, 2 tsps. sesame oil, miso and ginger in a small bowl. Whisk until well blended. Take a glass baking dish measuring 8"X8"X2" and place the fish in it. Pour the whisked miso mixture on the fish and turn to coat through. Keep aside to marinate at room temperature for 30 minutes.
- Line a baking dish with foil. Grease with a little oil. Gently place the fish on the foil and pour the mirin-miso marinade over it. Broil in preheated broiler for six minutes or until well cooked with brown specks.
- Place 1/4 cup green onions in a separate bowl along with 1 tbsp. vinegar, and 1 tsp. each of mirin and sesame oil. Mix well. Toss in the sunflower sprouts. Spoon the salad into four individual plates and top with fish. Garnish as desired, with the leftover green onions.

## Nutrition Information

- Calories: 263
- Total Carbohydrate: 9 g
- Cholesterol: 73 mg
- Total Fat: 7 g
- Fiber: 2 g
- Protein: 35 g
- Sodium: 951 mg
- Saturated Fat: 1 g

## 59. Miso-glazed Tuna Kebabs

*"This delicious meal of tuna kebabs is not like the typical and it's very pleasing. The tuna is wonderfully enhanced by the shiro miso with the help of the lush mayonnaise and mirin. The fish has a crispy edge to it thanks to the sugar content in the marinade. Once placed on the heated grill for a moment, it caramelizes!"*
*Serving: Makes 4 to 6 servings | Prep: 30m*

## Ingredients

- 1 cup white miso (also called shiro miso)

- 1/2 cup mirin (Japanese sweet rice wine)
- 1/2 cup sugar
- 1/4 cup water
- 1/2 cup mayonnaise
- 2 lbs. tuna steak, cut into 1-inch cubes
- 8 (12-inch) wooden skewers, soaked in water 30 minutes
- zucchini and snow-pea salad

## Direction

- Over moderate heat, stir water, sugar, mirin and miso in a small saucepan until the sugar dissolves. Move it away from the heat and stir in the mayonnaise then leave it to cool down to room temperature. Prepare a nonreactive shallow dish or sealable bag. Insert the tuna followed by the marinade. For a minimum of 1 hour, leave the bag to chill and marinate. Prepare high heat for gas and hot charcoal for cooking with direct heat over a grill. Spacing them out a little in between each piece, push the tuna onto the skewers. Place them atop a tray. Use generous amount of oil on the grill rack before grilling the skewers for around 4 minutes until the centre is just pink. During the process, flip it over once. When done, leave it to rest for 5 minutes.

## 60. Mixed Mushrooms Stroganoff

*"This modern adaptation of the classic pasta dish is a real treat for mushroom lovers. A healthier option of soy is used in place of the high-calorie sour cream, so you can enjoy it without too much guilt."*

## Ingredients

- 10 to 12 oz. ribbon-style noodles (see Note)
- 1 1/2 tbsps. light olive oil
- 1 large onion, chopped
- 12 to 16 oz. white mushrooms, sliced (see Tip)
- 4 to 6 oz. fresh shiitake mushrooms, sliced
- 4 to 6 oz. cremini or baby bella mushrooms, sliced

- 1/2 cup dry white wine, vegetable stock, or water
- One 12.3-oz. container silken tofu, puréed
- 1 tbsp. freshly squeezed lemon juice
- Freshly ground pepper
- 2 tbsps. nonhydrogenated margarine
- Salt, to taste, optional
- Minced fresh parsley for topping, optional
- Paprika for topping, optional
- Use spinach noodles, whole-grain ribbons made of quinoa or spelt flour, or pappardelle, broken into halves or thirds.

## Direction

- In plenty of speedily boil water, cook the noodles until al dente. In the meantime, in a stir-fry pan or big skillet, heat the oil. Over medium heat, sauté onion in the skillet until it turns golden before adding all the wine and mushrooms. Cover it up and let it simmer for about 10 minutes over low heat until the mushrooms turn tender. Stir in the lemon juice and tofu and heat gently until thoroughly heated before moving it away from the heat. Add pepper to season to taste. Drain the noodles and move it into a serving dish then mix the margarine in. If desired, season with salt. Layer each plate with a bed of noodles and pour some of the mushroom mixture over the top to serve. On each serving, decorate with a sprinkling of parsley and/or a dusting of paprika.
- To save time, use two 8-oz. packages presliced with mushrooms. Make sure they look fresh.

## Nutrition Information

- Calories: 265
- Total Carbohydrate: 35 g
- Cholesterol: 33 mg
- Total Fat: 9 g
- Fiber: 3 g
- Protein: 12 g
- Sodium: 43 mg
- Saturated Fat: 2 g

## 61. Mulled White Wine With Pear Brandy

*"This recipe is a mixture of white wine, star anise, cardamom, cinnamon, cloves, and ginger. Then fill the mixture with pear brandy. You can garnish the drink with a slice of Asian pear. A pear is known to soften as it absorbs the warm liquor and is also known to make drink a delicious one. You'll love it, especially when you serve it during a cozy evening indoors."*
*Serving: Serves 4*

### Ingredients

- One 750-ml bottle dry or off-dry white wine, preferably Riesling or Grüner Veltliner
- 1 piece star anise
- Two 1/4-inch-thick slices fresh ginger
- 3 green cardamom pods
- 3 whole cloves
- 3 to 4 tbsps. honey, or to taste
- 1/4 cup pear brandy, such as Poire Williams
- 4 slices Asian pear

### Direction

- In a heavy saucepan, combine wine, star anise, cloves, cardamom, 3 tsp. of honey (adjust later if necessary), and ginger. Bring it to simmer over medium heat while stirring the mixture occasionally. Remove it from the heat and let the wine mull for at least 15 minutes.
- You can taste and add more honey if you like. Place the wine back to a gentle heat and let it warm until it starts to steam. Turn off the heat and mix in the brandy.
- Distribute the mixture among 4 mugs or in heatproof glasses. You can add some whole spices and a slice of Asian pear in each mug if you like. Serve.

### Nutrition Information

- Calories: 253
- Total Carbohydrate: 26 g
- Total Fat: 0 g
- Fiber: 1 g
- Protein: 0 g
- Sodium: 2 mg
- Saturated Fat: 0 g

## 62. Mulled Wine

*"Make a cup of wholesome and warm beverage to cosy up during mid winter."*
*Serving: 8 | Ready in: 35m*

### Ingredients

- 1 bottle (750 ml) dry red wine, such as Merlot
- 1 cup water
- ¼ cup sugar, or to taste
- 3 whole cloves
- ¼ tsp. ground nutmeg
- ⅛ tsp. ground cardamom
- Pinch of ground allspice
- 2 strips fresh orange peel
- 2 strips fresh lemon peel

### Direction

- In a big saucepan, combine lemon peel, orange, allspice, cardamom, nutmeg, cloves, sugar, water and wine. Over low heat, let it simmer for 20 minutes.

### Nutrition Information

- Calories: 104 calories;
- Total Carbohydrate: 9 g
- Cholesterol: 0 mg
- Total Fat: 0 g
- Fiber: 0 g
- Protein: 0 g
- Sodium: 5 mg
- Sugar: 7 g
- Saturated Fat: 0 g

## 63. Mushroom Goat Cheese Pan Sauce

*"Mushroom is the most obvious choice of pan sauce that can't be missed out. In this one, shiitakes are chosen as they sauté much faster than others. This sauce is made richer with fresh goat cheese instead of butter or cream!"*

### Ingredients

- 1/4 cup canned low-sodium chicken broth
- 1/4 cup full-bodied red wine
- 1/2 lb. shiitake mushrooms, stems removed and discarded, caps sliced thin
- 2 tbsps. minced fresh parsley leaves
- 2 tbsps. fresh goat cheese

### Direction

- Use a measuring cup to estimate the wine and broth. In a skillet with nothing, fry the mushrooms for 2 to 3 minutes until they wilt. Mix goat cheese and parsley into the reduced liquid.

### Nutrition Information

- Calories: 90
- Total Carbohydrate: 9 g
- Cholesterol: 5 mg
- Total Fat: 3 g
- Fiber: 3 g
- Protein: 5 g
- Sodium: 74 mg
- Saturated Fat: 2 g

## 64. Mushrooms With Garlic And Madeira

*"Enjoy this as a snack or a first course by having it with toast, steak or omelette."*
*Serving: 4 to 6 side-dish servings*

### Ingredients

- 3 tbsps. olive oil
- 1 lb. whole small mushrooms or medium-size, halved
- 2 tbsps. chopped garlic
- 1/4 cup Madeira
- 1/2 cup whipping cream
- 1/4 cup thinly sliced fresh basil

### Direction

- Pour olive oil into a big, heavy skillet and heat over a high heat before adding the mushrooms. Sauté for around 6 minutes until browned but not juicy. Stir and cook garlic for around 30 seconds until the garlic becomes fragrant. Pour in the Madeira. Leave it cooking for a minute until it evaporates. Stir in the cut basil and whipping cream for around 1 minute until the mushrooms are coated with the sauce. Add pepper and salt to season. Serve.

### Nutrition Information

- Calories: 219
- Total Carbohydrate: 7 g
- Cholesterol: 33 mg
- Total Fat: 20 g
- Fiber: 1 g
- Protein: 4 g
- Sodium: 17 mg
- Saturated Fat: 7 g

## 65. Mussels With Coconut Curry Sauce

*"A different version of the Breton classic Mimosa that features coconut milk."*

### Ingredients

- 2 tbsps. (1/4 stick) butter
- 1/4 cup chopped shallots
- 2 tbsps. Madras curry powder
- 1 14-oz. can unsweetened coconut milk
- 1 1/2 cups dry white wine
- 3 tbsps. fresh lemon juice

- 2 small bay leaves
- 2 lbs. black mussels, scrubbed, debearded
- Chopped fresh parsley

## Direction

- On medium heat, melt butter in a big saucepan; put in curry powder and shallots. Cook and stir for a minute until aromatic. Put in bay leaves, coconut milk, lemon juice, and wine; let it simmer for 10mins then add mussels. Turn heat up and cover the pot. Boil for 6mins until the mussels open. Divide mussels among four bowls using tongs and remove the unopened mussels. Boil the sauce for two minutes until slightly thick, stir from time to time. Sprinkle pepper and salt; remove bay leaves. Ladle sauce over the mussels; garnish with parsley.

## Nutrition Information

- Calories: 254
- Total Carbohydrate: 9 g
- Cholesterol: 39 mg
- Total Fat: 16 g
- Fiber: 1 g
- Protein: 15 g
- Sodium: 335 mg
- Saturated Fat: 12 g

## 66. My Favorite Brisket (not Too Gedempte Fleysch)

*"If you want the undying affection of your in-laws, this great tasting classic brisket is what you should prepare for them. The recipe may have been in my family for many years, but it can easily be spiced up with a little tweak here and there. For one, you can put in a jar of sun-dried tomatoes – packed in oil or dry – to intensify the flavor. You can also include a 2-inch knob of ginger and a few strips of lemon zest into the pot."*
*Serving: Serves 10*

## Ingredients

- 2 tsps. salt
- Freshly ground black pepper
- 1 (5-lb.) brisket of beef, shoulder roast of beef, chuck roast, or end of steak
- 1 clove garlic, peeled
- 2 tbsps. vegetable oil
- 3 onions, peeled and diced
- 1 (10-oz.) can tomatoes
- 2 cups red wine
- 2 stalks celery with the leaves, chopped
- 1 bay leaf
- 1 sprig thyme
- 1 sprig rosemary
- 1/4 cup chopped parsley
- 6 to 8 carrots, peeled and sliced on the diagonal

## Direction

- Preheat the oven to 325°F. Season the brisket with salt and pepper to taste and massage the garlic. Sear brisket in oil and put it on top of the onions with the fat side up inside a big casserole. Layer with rosemary, thyme, bay leaf, celery, tomatoes and red wine over the top. Cover it up and bake for about 3 hours in the oven. Baste the meat with pan juices. Mix in the carrots and parsley and bake without any cover on until the carrots are cooked, about 30 minutes. Stick a fork into the brisket to test the doneness. When the fork has a light pull as it is being removed from the meat, it is at the desired state of fork-tender.

- In order to skim the fat off the surface of the gravy, it's advisable to prepare it in advance and just keep it refrigerated. Before serving, preheat the oven to 350°F and reheat the gravy in a pan on the stove. Some people like to strain the gravy but others prefer to skip this step to keep the onions because they are delicious. Get rid of all the visible fat from the cold brisket before placing it on a cutting board with the fat side down. Look for the grain that is, the muscle lines of the brisket and use a sharp knife to cut across the grain.

- In a roasting pan, set the sliced brisket down then pour the hot gravy over it. Cover and reheat for 30 minutes in the oven.

## Nutrition Information

- Calories: 610
- Total Carbohydrate: 11 g
- Cholesterol: 141 mg
- Total Fat: 39 g
- Fiber: 3 g
- Protein: 47 g
- Sodium: 617 mg
- Saturated Fat: 15 g

## 67. New York Sour

*"Perform a dry shake – where you shake the drink ingredients and egg white without any ice – as this doesn't dilute the drink but still gets the whites foamy."*
*Serving: makes 2*

### Ingredients

- 1 large egg white
- 4 oz. rye whiskey
- 1 1/2 oz. fresh lemon juice
- 1 oz. simple syrup
- 1 oz. full-bodied red wine

### Direction

- In a cocktail shaker, shake a combination of lemon juice, whiskey, egg white and simple syrup for 1 minute or until frothy. Put ice into the shaker and shake it for 30 seconds or until the outside turns frosty. Strain the mixture into 2 coupe glasses. Pour 1/2 oz. of wine gently over the back of a spoon held a little above each drink's surface. This is to ensure that the wine stays afloat on the top.

### Nutrition Information

- Calories: 205
- Total Carbohydrate: 12 g
- Total Fat: 0 g
- Fiber: 0 g
- Protein: 2 g
- Sodium: 36 mg
- Saturated Fat: 0 g

## 68. Nose-warmer Punch

*Serving: Makes about 12 1/2 cups, serving 12.*

### Ingredients

- 3 bottles dry red wine
- 1 1/2 cups brandy
- 1 1/2 cups sugar
- 3 cinnamon sticks
- 8 whole cloves
- 3 small lemons, zest scored lengthwise if desired with a channel knife and fruit sliced thin crosswise

### Direction

- Cook and stir cloves, wine, cinnamon, brandy, and sugar in a big pot for two minutes into bare simmer; mix in lemon slices. Spoon mixture into heat-proof containers.

### Nutrition Information

- Calories: 486
- Total Carbohydrate: 46 g
- Total Fat: 0 g
- Fiber: 1 g
- Protein: 0 g
- Sodium: 13 mg
- Saturated Fat: 0 g

## 69. Orange And Yogurt Parfaits With Red Wine Caramel

*"Fancy an ice cream dessert? Try these eye catching parfaits made with low fat yogurt served with fresh oranges and topped with red wine."*
*Serving: Makes 4 Servings | Prep: 10m*

### Ingredients

- 1 cup sugar
- 3 whole star anise
- Pinch of cream of tartar

- 1/2 cup dry, fruity red wine, such as Syrah, divided
- 2 large oranges
- 1 1/2 cups low-fat plain Greek yogurt
- 1/2 cup toasted hazelnuts, almonds, or pistachios, coarsely chopped
- Fresh mint leaves

## Direction

- In a medium saucepan place 3 tbsps. of water. Stir in the cream of tartar, sugar, and star anise. Cook on medium high heat until the ingredients come to a boil. Swirl occasionally and continue cooking for eight minutes until the sugar caramelizes and takes on the colour of dark maple syrup. Take the casserole off the heat and very carefully, stir in 1/4 cup red wine until the caramelized sugar dissolves. Pour in the rest of the 1/4 cup red wine and let boil for 1/2 minute until the sugar is completely dissolved. Let fully cool. Cover and refrigerate. Slightly warm before using.
- Peel the oranges with a sharp knife and remove the white pith. Slice the oranges in rings less than 1/4" thick.
- Take individual glass jars and line the bottom with one or two orange rings. Pour a good one tbsp. of red wine caramel over them. Spoon a small helping of yogurt over this and sprinkle nuts. Repeat the process until you have three layers. Drizzle a little caramel and garnish with mint leaves. You can make these parfaits 1/2 hour ahead of serving. Cover and store in refrigerator if they are not to be served immediately.

## 70. Orange Wine

*Serving: Makes about 7 cups*

## Ingredients

- 2 lbs. (about 4) oranges, each cut into 16 pieces
- Two 750-ml bottles dry white wine
- 1 cup sugar

- 1/4 cup Cognac
- Garnish: long strips of orange zest removed with a vegetable peeler

## Direction

- Mix wine and oranges in a big bowl then use a plastic wrap to cover firmly; refrigerate for five days. Remove the oranges; stir in Cognac and sugar until the sugar dissolves. Line sieve with rinsed and squeezed double-thick cheesecloth, strain mixture into the bowl. Transfer wine into corked decorative containers. Add a strip of orange zest in every container; chill for a week. Refrigerated, it can last for three months.

## Nutrition Information

- Calories: 425
- Total Carbohydrate: 58 g
- Total Fat: 0 g
- Fiber: 4 g
- Protein: 2 g
- Sodium: 13 mg
- Saturated Fat: 0 g

## 71. Orange-honey Sauce

*"To brighten up your day, this buttery goodness will help warm your soul!"*
*Serving: Makes about 1 1/3 cups*

## Ingredients

- 1 cup Essencia (orange Muscat wine) or late-harvest Riesling
- 2/3 cup chopped shallots (about 4 large)
- 1/2 cup orange juice
- 1 tbsp. honey
- 2 1/2 cups chicken stock or canned low-salt chicken broth
- 3 tbsps. chilled butter, cut into 3 pieces

## Direction

- In a heavy midsized saucepan, mix the initial four ingredients. For around 12 minutes, let the mixture simmer at a moderate heat until it reduces into 1/2 cup. Insert the stock and continue simmering for the next 20 minutes. Proceed until the sauce reduces into 1-1/4 cups. Prepare to beat the butter in one at a time, making sure that one has already melted before continuing. Add dashes of pepper and salt.

## Nutrition Information

- Calories: 340
- Total Carbohydrate: 29 g
- Cholesterol: 41 mg
- Total Fat: 16 g
- Fiber: 1 g
- Protein: 7 g
- Sodium: 329 mg
- Saturated Fat: 9 g

## 72. Orange-vanilla Sundaes With Dates And Orange Muscat

*"Enjoy this tasty bowl of sherbet in the summer heat!"*
*Serving: Makes 6 servings*

## Ingredients

- 3/4 cup pecans, chopped and toasted
- 3/4 cup Essencia or other orange Muscat dessert wine
- 1/2 cup heavy cream
- 2 pints premium-quality vanilla ice cream
- 12 large Deglet or Medjool dates, pitted and chopped
- 2 pints orange or tangerine sherbet
- 6 sprigs fresh mint

## Direction

- Combine wine and pecans in a small bowl and whip the cream in a big bowl until it holds soft peaks. Prepare 6 parfait glasses or glass serving dishes then place one scoop of vanilla ice cream inside every single one. Layer each glass with a tbsp. of pecan mixture and a tbsp. of dates. Over each of the glasses, add the remaining pecan mixture and 1 scoop of sherbet. Top each glass off with the rest of the dates and whipped cream and finish off with a twig of mint as garnish. Serve at once.

## Nutrition Information

- Calories: 618
- Total Carbohydrate: 88 g
- Cholesterol: 67 mg
- Total Fat: 28 g
- Fiber: 6 g
- Protein: 7 g
- Sodium: 121 mg
- Saturated Fat: 12 g

## 73. Oxtail Bourguinonne

*Serving: 6 servings | Prep: 1h*

## Ingredients

- 8 slices fatty bacon, chopped
- Olive oil
- 3 large fresh Italian parsley sprigs
- 3 large fresh thyme sprigs
- 2 large fresh bay leaves, bruised
- 1 tbsp. plus 1 1/2 cups all purpose flour
- 1 tbsp. butter
- 1/4 tsp. ground nutmeg
- 4 to 4 1/4 lbs. meaty oxtail pieces, trimmed of excess fat
- 2 cups chopped onions
- 1 cup diced carrot plus 6 medium carrots, cut into 2-inch chunks
- 4 large garlic cloves, peeled; 1 minced, 3 left whole
- 1 3/4 cups beef broth
- 1 1/2 cups red Burgundy wine (such as Beaujolais)
- 1 lb. crimini (baby bella) mushrooms, cut into 1/4-inch-thick slices

- 12 small (1-inch-diameter) shallots, blanched 1 minute, peeled

## Direction

- Heat a big heavy pot over medium high heat and cook bacon. When brown and crisp, transfer to a platter using a slotted spoon to drain any liquid. Transfer drippings in another bowl. Place about six tbsps. of the drippings back in the pot. Add a little olive oil if the liquid runs short of six tbsps.. Put bacon aside. Prepare bouquet garni of parsley, bay leaves and thyme. In a separate bowl, combine butter and one tbsp. four to a smooth paste.
- In a medium bowl, whisk together 1 1/2 cups flour with 2 tsps. salt, nutmeg, and 1/2 tsp. freshly ground black pepper. Toss oxtails, in small batches, to seasoned flour to coat thoroughly.
- Place pot on medium high heat and heat the bacon drippings. Add oxtails in batches and cook for six minutes by batches until the oxtails are brown all over. Remove from pot and transfer to a bowl.
- Add diced carrot, chopped onions, and minced garlic to the pot and cook for about five minutes or until the onions soften. Return the oxtails to the pot along with any juices. Add bouquet garni. Add wine and broth and boil. When it comes to a boil, reduce heat, cover pot and simmer for three hours or until the meat is tender. Adjust heat if necessary to maintain a gentle simmer. Add shallots, mushrooms, carrot chunks, and whole cloves of garlic. Increase heat. When the pot starts boiling, cover it and allow to simmer for another 45 minutes, until the vegetables and meat are tender.
- Skim fat from surface of stew and stir in the flour paste. Allow to simmer, uncovered, for about eight minutes, until the sauce thickens a little. Stir occasionally. Season with pepper and salt. This stew can be made one day ahead. Refrigerate without covering the pot. When cold, cover and allow to remain in refrigerator. Before serving, warm the stew on low heat.

## Nutrition Information

- Calories: 1343
- Total Carbohydrate: 59 g
- Cholesterol: 236 mg
- Total Fat: 85 g
- Fiber: 7 g
- Protein: 74 g
- Sodium: 600 mg
- Saturated Fat: 31 g

## 74. Pan-glazed Fish With Citrus And Soy

*"The marinade works well with both mild and intense fish, choose to your liking. For a heavier and meatier fish, go for the swordfish and for a milder fish, go for bass or cod."*
*Serving: Makes 4 servings*

## Ingredients

- 4 (4-oz.) pieces Spanish mackerel fillet, any bones removed
- 1 tbsp. fresh grapefruit juice
- 1 tbsp. fresh lime juice
- 2 tbsps. sake
- 3 tbsps. mirin (Japanese sweet rice wine)
- 3 tbsps. Japanese light soy sauce
- 1 tbsp. water
- 2 tsps. sugar
- 2 tsps. vegetable oil
- Garnish: lime slices

## Direction

- Prepare a ceramic dish or glass with flat bottom that's big enough to place the fillets out in a layer. Insert the fish. In a little bowl, mix the juices together. In another little bowl, blend sake with 1 tbsp. of the mixed juices and layer this atop the fillets. At room temperature, leave it to marinate for 10 minutes. Combine 2 tbsps. of soy sauce and mirin to be poured atop the fillets. For another 5 minutes, let it marinate at room temperature. If desired, it can be kept for an hour inside of a refrigerator. Remove the fish out of the marinade then dry it through patting. Get rid of the marinade.

- In a small bowl, combine soy sauce, sugar, water and remaining 1 tbsp. of each of the mixed juices.
- Over medium-high heat, heat the oil in a heavy 12-inch non-stick skillet. Once it's hot enough but not smoking, start sautéing the fillets for a minute or two with the skin side down until they turn golden brown and crispy. Flip the fillets over and continue sautéing for another minute until it browns. Pour the soy mixture into the skillet. Cook for around 3 minutes until the fillets are thoroughly cooked and the sauce reduces to a glaze. During the cooking process, swirl the skillet around from time to time. In the case that the sauce diminishes before fish is done cooking, feel free to add in an extra tbsp. of water. Repeating if needed until the fish is done.

## Nutrition Information

- Calories: 220
- Total Carbohydrate: 4 g
- Cholesterol: 86 mg
- Total Fat: 10 g
- Fiber: 0 g
- Protein: 23 g
- Sodium: 451 mg
- Saturated Fat: 2 g

## 75. Pan-seared Five-spice Duck Breast With Balsamic Jus

*"When I made duck for the first time ever, it was a painful experience that took three days and the result was a sad portion. Since then, I've found a solution in the form of duck breasts. They are perfect as they are less fatty than the thighs or legs. Additionally, they barely shrink after the preparation period. You can make a special order them or find them in the frozen section of most supermarkets. This recipe calls for intense searing, which turns the skin crispy and nice while the aromatic five-spice powder gives the duck a striking flair. Using a mixture of balsamic vinegar and wine to deglaze the pan creates the ideal simple sauce. A sophisticated Russian River Valley Pinot Noir is a great match for this duck dish. Serve duck with Pepper Salad, Prosciutto and French Lentil."*
*Serving: Serves 6*

## Ingredients

- 1 large garlic clove, finely chopped
- 1 tbsp grated peeled fresh ginger
- 2 tsp five-spice powder
- 1 tsp salt
- 1/2 tsp freshly ground pepper
- 4 single duck breasts
- 1 tbsp extra-virgin olive oil
- 1/4 cup/60 ml dry red wine
- 2 tbsp balsamic vinegar

## Direction

- Combine the pepper, salt, five-spice powder, ginger and garlic in a big, sturdy plastic bag that seals itself. Before sealing, insert the duck breasts. Refrigerate for a minimum of 1 hour or overnight. An hour before ready to cook, get it out of the refrigerator.
- Preheat the oven to 400°F (200°C or Gas 6). Over moderately high heat, heat the olive oil in a big ovenproof frying pan until it shimmers.
- Sear duck breast for 5 minutes with its skin side down then turn and sear for 5 minutes on the other side. Move the pan into the oven and roast for 5 minutes to get medium-rare. Move

the duck breast onto a plate and maintain it at a warm temperature.

- To make a balsamic jus, discard the fats on the pan. Over moderately high heat, stir wine into the pan and use it to scrape up the browned bits attached to the bottom of the pan. Continue cooking until the wine reduces the by half before adding the balsamic vinegar. Cook for a few more minutes to reduce. Diagonally cut the duck breasts into slices. Before serving, drizzle the balsamic jus.

## Nutrition Information

- Calories: 173
- Total Carbohydrate: 2 g
- Cholesterol: 85 mg
- Total Fat: 7 g
- Fiber: 0 g
- Protein: 22 g
- Sodium: 304 mg
- Saturated Fat: 2 g

---

## 76. Panna Cotta With Strawberry-vin Santo Sauce

*"The original panna cotta was served topped with honey and pine nuts and a luscious strawberry sauce laced with Vin Santo."*
*Serving: Makes 10 servings*

## Ingredients

- 1/4 cup cold water
- 4 tsps. unflavored gelatin
- 4 cups whipping cream
- 1 cup sugar
- 1 tbsp. orange blossom honey
- 1/4 tsp. vanilla extract
- 1 tbsp. Vin Santo,* Muscat wine or cream Sherry
- 2 cups pine nuts (about 9 oz.)
- Strawberry-Vin Santo Sauce
- Additional pine nuts

## Direction

- Sprinkle gelatin over 1/4 cup water in a metal bowl. Set aside for ten minutes until the gelatin is soft. Heat some water in a pot until it begins to simmer. Place the bowl of gelatine in the pot and stir gently for about a minute until the gelatine is dissolved completely.
- In a large heavy pot, place the sugar, honey, cream and vanilla. Place over heat and bring to a boil, stirring all the time to dissolve the sugar. Turn off the heat. Whisk in the Vin Santo and the gelatin until the mixture is completely blended.
- In ten medium sized custard cups, equally divide the two cups of pine nuts and the prepared cream mixture. Place cups in refrigerator to chill overnight. When ready to serve, place the cups of panna cotta briefly in a small bowl of warm water. Lift from water and gently loosen sides by running a small knife around the inside of the cups. Gently invert the cups onto serving plates. Drizzle sauce over the panna cotta and garnish with pine nuts. Serve cold.

---

## 77. Peach Prosecco

*"This cocktail recipe was created by a bartender from a place called The Windsor in Phoenix. It has a true peach-based liqueur for a pure peach flavor. The use of one of the following: Massenez Crème de Peche, Rothman & Winter Orchard Peach Liqueur or Sathenay Crème de Peche de Vigne Liqueur are highly recommended."*
*Serving: Makes 1 drink*

## Ingredients

- 1 oz. vodka
- 1 oz. peach liqueur
- 1 oz. Prosecco
- 1/2 oz. lemon juice
- 1/2 oz. peach nectar
- 2 dashes Fee Brothers peach bitters (optional)
- Peach wedge

### Direction

- In a cocktail shaker, mix peach nectar, lemon juice, Prosecco, peach liqueur, vodka and bitters (optional). Fill shaker with ice then strongly shake for 20 seconds until mixed completely. Strain in a cooled champagne coupe then top with a peach wedge.

---

## 78. Peach White-wine Sangria

*Serving: Makes 8 to 10 drinks | Prep: 15m*

### Ingredients

- 1 cup loosely packed fresh basil leaves plus 8 to 10 sprigs
- 3/4 cup sugar
- 1/4 cup fresh lemon juice
- 2 cans peach nectar (23 fluid oz. total)
- 1 (750-ml) bottle chilled dry white wine
- 1 large peach (peeled if desired), diced

### Direction

- In a small pot, put lemon juice, sugar, and basil leaves; use a wooden spoon to mash and bruise leaves. Pour in one can of nectar and let it simmer, stir until the sugar dissolves. Take off heat and set aside for 5mins. Strain the mixture using a medium-mesh sieve into a heatproof pitcher to remove the basil leaves. Mix in basil sprigs, wine, leftover can of nectar, and peach. Refrigerate for an hour to a whole day while covered. Serve with ice.

### Nutrition Information

- Calories: 223
- Total Carbohydrate: 40 g
- Total Fat: 0 g
- Fiber: 1 g
- Protein: 1 g
- Sodium: 13 mg
- Saturated Fat: 0 g

## 79. Peaches And Raspberries In Spiced White Wine

*"This dessert is a peachy, fruity, boozy delight."*
*Serving: Serves 8*

### Ingredients

- 1 bottle (750ml) Italian dry white wine, such as Pinot Bianco or Pinot Grigio
- 1/2 cup sugar
- 4 3/4 x 2-inch orange peel strips (orange part only)
- 3 cinnamon sticks
- 6 peaches
- 2 1/2-pint baskets raspberries
- Biscotti

### Direction

- In a small saucepan, combine cinnamon, orange peel, sugar and 1 cup of wine. Over low heat, stir until the sugar dissolves then turn the heat up. Let it simmer for 15 minutes before moving it away from the heat and adding the remainder of the wine. In a big pot of boiling water, blanch the peaches for 20 seconds. Use a slotted spoon to transfer the peaches into a bowl of cold water then drain it. Use a little sharp knife to peel the skin off. Cut the peaches up into slices and put them in a big bowl then add the wine mixture and raspberries. Cover and keep it in the fridge for a minimum of 1 hour. (This can be prepped 6 hours in advance. Stir it from time to time.) Among the glass goblets, distribute the fruit and wine. Serve together with biscotti.

## 80. Pear Brandy Cocktails

*"What's remarkable about this drink? The wonderful smell of pear, the fun little sugar cube and the fact that it goes well with light snacks."*
*Serving: Makes 6 drinks | Prep: 5m*

### Ingredients

- 6 sugar cubes
- 6 tsps. pear brandy
- 1 chilled 750-ml bottle Prosecco

### Direction

- Prepare six Champagne flutes. In every one, insert around 2/3 cup of Prosecco, 1 tsp. of pear brandy and a sugar cube.

### Nutrition Information

- Calories: 129
- Total Carbohydrate: 7 g
- Protein: 0 g
- Sodium: 6 mg

## 81. Pears Bordelaise

*Serving: Serves 6*

### Ingredients

- 1 cup red Bordeaux wine
- 2 cups sugar
- 6 peeled whole pears
- 1 jar apple jelly

### Direction

- Place sugar and wine in a pan. Boil until sugar melts. Gently poach pears in this well blended syrup, turning them occasionally so they are evenly cooked and well colored. Baste pears by spooning liquid on them. When the pears are tender take pan off the heat, and cool. Add jelly to the syrup in the pan and cook for a few minutes. Pour this syrup on the pears and chill well before serving.

### Nutrition Information

- Calories: 536
- Total Carbohydrate: 131 g
- Total Fat: 0 g
- Fiber: 6 g
- Protein: 1 g
- Sodium: 20 mg
- Saturated Fat: 0 g

## 82. Peppered Lamb Burgers With "hot Tomato" Jam

*Serving: 4 burgers*

### Ingredients

- 4 cups ripe tomatoes, peeled, cored, and roughly chopped (for best results, use a variety of tomatoes)
- 1/3 cup sugar
- 3 tbsps. finely minced fresh ginger
- 2 tbsps. unseasoned rice vinegar
- 1 tsp. hot pepper sauce
- 3 tbsps. fresh basil, cut into chiffonade
- Salt
- 1 1/3 lbs. freshly ground lamb
- 2 tbsps. five-peppercorn blend, cracked or very coarsely ground
- 1 garlic clove, finely minced
- 2 tbsps. sesame oil
- 1/4 cup Merlot
- Salt
- Olive oil, for brushing on the grill rack
- 4 hamburger buns, split
- 4 red leaf lettuce leaves

### Direction

- In a charcoal grill, heat to medium-hot fire with cover or heat gas grill to medium-high.
- Taste and add the rest of pepper sauce to taste. Cook the mixture continuously until turns to

the consistency of jam. Take out from the heat. Put on the side and allow to cool. Add in basil into cooled mixture; stir. Sprinkle salt to taste. Put on the side.

- Preparation of jam: Mix together sugar, 1/2 tsp. pepper sauce, tomatoes, ginger, and vinegar in a nonreactive saucepan that's flame-proof. Put the pan with the mixture into the grill rack, allowing the mixture to simmer slowly. Simmer continuously while occasionally stirring the mixture, moving off and on the heat as needed until reduced into half for about 30 minutes.
- Transfer pan into the coolest portion of the rack. Cook continuously for 15 minutes more.
- Preparation of patties: In a big bowl, mix together peppercorn blend, Merlot, lamb, garlic, and sesame oil. Sprinkle salt to season. Combine well by handling the meat little by little to prevent compacting. Equally, divide mixture to 4 portions and mold portions into patties fitted to the buns.
- Use olive oil to paint grill rack. Put the patties on the oiled rack and cook with cover, flipping once, until grilled in your preference; about 4 minutes a side for medium-rare. Put buns, seam side down on last few minutes at the outer sides of grilling rack until lightly toasted.
- Assembling burgers: Add the tomato jam on the slice side of the bread; spread. Put patty and lettuce leaf on each bottom of bun then place the top bun over. Serve.

## 83. Pineapple Sangria

*"Try this sangria drink that you can tweak based on your preference. Drink! Drink! Drink!"*
*Serving: 8 | Prep: 25m | Ready in: 8h25m*

## Ingredients

- 2 (750 milliliter) bottles Sauvignon Blanc
- 2 cups pineapple juice
- 1 cup triple sec
- 1/2 cup brandy (optional)
- 1/2 cup chopped fresh pineapple
- 1/2 cup chopped orange
- 1 lemon, seeded and chopped
- 1/4 cup chopped lime
- 2 cups lemon-lime flavored carbonated beverage (such as 7-Up®)

## Direction

- Combine together triple sec, pineapple juice, brandy, and Sauvignon Blanc into a big pitcher. Put in lemon, orange, lime, and sliced pineapple. Keep in the refrigerator with cover for 8 hours to overnight.
- Mix in lemon-lime soda. Serve.

## Nutrition Information

- Calories: 383 calories;
- Total Carbohydrate: 38.5 g
- Cholesterol: 0 mg
- Total Fat: 0.3 g
- Protein: 0.8 g
- Sodium: 26 mg

## 84. Plum Sherbert With Orange Juice And Plum Wine

*"It's a beautiful pink dessert that is refreshing and light. Plums with dark purple flesh or skin will give lovely color to the sherbet. Serve it together with a pot of green tea."*
*Serving: Makes 6 servings*

## Ingredients

- 5 firm but ripe plums, halved, pitted, cut into large chunks
- 1/2 cup sugar
- 1/4 cup water
- 1/2 cup fresh orange juice
- 1/2 cup light corn syrup
- 2 tbsps. Japanese plum wine*
- 2 tsps. grated orange peel
- 1 tsp. fresh lemon juice
- 1 tsp. vanilla extract
- Large pinch of salt

- 1 cup whipping cream
- Additional Japanese plum wine

## Direction

- In a heavy and medium saucepan, mix the sugar, a 1/4 cup of water, and plums. Let the mixture cook over medium-low heat for 12 minutes until the liquid is syrupy and the plums are tender. Allow it to cool completely.
- Pour the plum mixture into the processor and puree it until almost smooth. Mix in orange peel, orange juice, a pinch of salt, corn syrup, vanilla extract, lemon juice, and plum wine. Add the cream. Process the mixture until well-blended. Transfer the blended mixture into the ice cream maker and process it according to the manufacturer's directions. Transfer the mixture into the covered container and freeze for 3 hours until firm. (Take note that the sherbet can be prepared 2 days ahead. Just keep it frozen.) Spoon the sherbet into bowls. Drizzle sherbet with additional plum wine. Serve.

## Nutrition Information

- Calories: 303
- Total Carbohydrate: 49 g
- Cholesterol: 44 mg
- Total Fat: 13 g
- Fiber: 1 g
- Protein: 1 g
- Sodium: 93 mg
- Saturated Fat: 8 g

## 85. Poached Pears With Sweet Wine And Fruit Confetti

*Serving: Serves 6*

## Ingredients

- 6 small firm but ripe Anjou pears, peeled
- 3 1/2 cups sweet white or red wine (such as Moscato) from 1-liter bottle
- 2 cups pear nectar
- 1 cinnamon stick, broken in half
- 1 vanilla bean, split lengthwise
- 1 1/2 tsps. arrowroot
- 1/2 cup chopped peeled kiwi
- 1/2 cup chopped peeled seeded cantaloupe
- 1/2 cup quartered hulled strawberries
- Fresh mint sprigs

## Direction

- Carefully remove the core from the bottom ends of the pears. Place the pear nectar, cinnamon and wine in a big pot. Scrape the seeds from the vanilla bean and add the bean. Simmer and add the prepared pears. Remember to keep the pears half submerged in the liquid. Continue cooking on medium-low heat, turning the pears halfway through, for ten minutes or until they are tender. Remove from heat, turn out the cooking liquid along with the pears into a big bowl and let it cool completely.
- Transfer the liquid back into the pot. In a small bowl, combine the arrowroot powder with 2 tbsps. of the liquid. Return casserole to the heat and allow it to boil for approximately 12 minutes, stirring occasionally. Continue boiling till the sauce thickens and reduces to 2 cups. Remove from heat and keep aside to cool completely. Cover and refrigerate. Remember to bring the sauce to room temperature before serving.
- Serve in shallow bowls, placing pears over the sauce. Decorate attractively with cantaloupe, kiwi and strawberries and garnish with mint before serving.

## 86. Porcini Mushroom Sauce

*"This dish is perfect with roast chicken or steak."*
*Serving: Makes about 2 cups*

## Ingredients

- 1 1/2 oz. dried porcini mushrooms

- 1 cup warm water
- 2 tbsps. olive oil
- 1 cup chopped onion
- 2 garlic cloves, minced
- 1/2 cup dry Marsala
- 1/2 cup dry white wine
- 1 tsp. minced fresh rosemary
- 1 cup chicken stock or canned low-salt chicken broth
- 1 cup beef stock or canned beef broth
- 1 tbsp. butter, room temperature
- 1 tbsp. all purpose flour

## Direction

- Put porcini mushrooms in a bowl with a cup of warm water; set aside for half an hour until the mushrooms are soft. Drain the mushrooms and squeeze out the excess liquid back in the bowl; reserve the mushroom liquid. Place the drained mushrooms in a separate small bowl.
- On medium heat, heat oil in a big heavy pot; add garlic and onion. Sauté for 15mins until the onion is brown; pour in white wine and Marsala. Turn the heat up and boil for 7mins until most of the liquid has evaporated. Put it both stocks, mushrooms, rosemary, and the reserved liquid from mushroom except any of the remaining sediments. Boil for 15mins until the liquid reduces to two cups.
- In a small bowl, blend flour and butter together; stir into the mushroom. Let it simmer for 2mins until the sauce is thick. Sprinkle pepper and salt to season.

## Nutrition Information

- Calories: 206
- Total Carbohydrate: 19 g
- Cholesterol: 9 mg
- Total Fat: 11 g
- Fiber: 2 g
- Protein: 5 g
- Sodium: 213 mg
- Saturated Fat: 3 g

# 87. Pork And Chive Dumplings With Dried Shrimp

*"Regardless of whether it's fried (pot stickers) or steamed, these traditional pleated dumplings (typically Chinese) are always amazing. If you don't have a lot of time on hand, you can go for readymade round gyoza wrappers (otherwise known as pot sticker wrapper or dumpling). They can be found in most Asian markets or the frozen section of grocery stores."*
*Serving: Makes about 40 dumplings*

## Ingredients

- 2 cups all-purpose flour
- 3/4 tsp. salt
- 2 tsps. dried shrimp
- 2 tsps. Chinese rice wine, such as Shaoxing, or medium-dry Sherry
- 6 oz. cabbage (1/4 medium head), roughly chopped
- 1/2 tsp. kosher salt
- 1 lb. ground pork
- 1 bunch golden or green garlic chives, finely chopped (1/2 cup)
- 2 scallions (green parts only), thinly sliced on the diagonal
- 1 clove garlic, finely chopped
- 1/8 tsp. fresh ginger, finely grated
- 3 tbsps. soy sauce
- 1 tbsp. oyster sauce
- 1 tbsp. sugar
- 1/2 tsp. Asian sesame oil
- 1 large egg, beaten
- 1/4 tsp. freshly ground black pepper
- 1 heaping tbsp. cornstarch
- 4 1/2 tbsps. vegetable oil
- 1/4 cup soy sauce
- 1/3 cup unseasoned rice vinegar
- 1 tsp. Sriracha (Southeast Asian chile sauce)
- 1 scallion (green part only), thinly sliced on the diagonal
- 2 large baking sheets; large saucepan or large nonstick skillet with tight-fitting lid; metal or bamboo steamer (if steaming dumplings)

## Direction

- Combine 1 cup of boiling water, salt and flour in a big bowl to make dough. Mix with a wooden spoon until the dough forms shaggy ball. Move it onto a lightly floured surface and knead for 6 to 8 minutes until smooth and glossy (Kneading time would be shorter if you will use an electric mixer fitted with dough hook to mix and knead it.) Use plastic wrap to seal it up lightly and give it 20 minutes to stand at room temperature.
- While dough rest, make filling while combining all of the ingredients in a large bowl and knead mixture gently with your hands in bowl until just combined. Keep refrigerated until ready to use.
- Roll out of the wrappers. Use paper towels to line a big baking sheet and dust it lightly with flour. Break the dough up evenly into 3 pieces. Use the palms of your hands to roll every piece into a 3/4-inch diameter log on a lightly floured surface. Cut each one of the logs up into sections that are 1-inch in length with a floured knife.
- Get 1 pinch from the dough section and turn it into a circle. On a floured surface, use a floured rolling pin to roll it into a 4-inch round diameter. Move it onto a baking sheet and do the same with all the rest of the dough sections. Stack each round onto the floured paper towel to make layers.
- Use paper towels to line second big baking sheet and dust it lightly with flour for filling and pleating dumplings. With 1 wrapper on the palm of a hand, hold gently wet the edge of the wrapper with a fingertip that has been dipped in water. In the centre of the wrapper, put 1 heaping tbsp. of filling. Fold the wrapper in half without sealing the edges, cupping half-moon with the open side up in between the fingers and thumb. Gently tamp the filling down with the other hand to keep the edge of the wrapper filling-free.
- Start pinching the edges of wrapper together with the forefinger of left hand and the thumb. At the same time, use the right hand's thumb to push 1 edge into tiny pleats. Across the entire semicircle, continue pinching and pleating until the wrapper is sealed (the un-pleated side will curve on its own). Set dumpling, sealed edge up, on baking sheet and repeat with remaining wrappers and filling.
- For steaming: Bring 1-1/2 inches of water in a big saucepan with a tight-fitting lid to a boil. Oil the metal steamer lightly (use cabbage leaves to line in order to prevent sticking if using bamboo) and set it in the pan. Organize the dumplings on the steamer with the sealed edges facing up then cover it up. Steam until the wrappers turn slightly translucent and the filling is firm.
- For pan-frying: Over moderately high heat, heat 1-1/2 tbsps. of vegetable oil in a large lidded non-stick frying pan until hot but not smoking yet. Insert 13 to 14 dumplings with the pleated side facing up and no part of it touching one another. Immediately pour adequate amount of cold water in right away until it comes halfway up the sides of dumplings. Use care, oil may splatter. Cover it up and cook for about 10 minutes. They are ready when the bottoms of the dumplings turn golden and crisp and the liquid has evaporated (Check the bottoms by lifting and loosening the edges with a spatula. If needed, replace lid and continue cooking for, checking after 1 or 2 minutes). Move the dumplings onto a platter with the crispy sides facing up. Make sure it stays warm. Do the exact same thing with the remaining 2 batches of dumplings. As the dumplings cook, stir all the ingredients together in a medium bowl to make the dipping sauce. Serve this together with the dumplings while they are warm.

## Nutrition Information

- Calories: 75
- Total Carbohydrate: 6 g
- Cholesterol: 13 mg
- Total Fat: 4 g
- Fiber: 0 g
- Protein: 3 g

- Sodium: 180 mg
- Saturated Fat: 1 g

## 88. Pork Chops With Apples

*"This recipe gives you a great excuse to consume apples in a way that's different from usual. A sweet fruit together with meat, this dish is completely nutritious and delicious all at the same time."*
*Serving: Serves 4*

## Ingredients

- 4 medium pork chops (you can substitute veal chops if you prefer)
- 4 whole cloves
- 1/2 cup dry white wine or vermouth
- 4 celery leaves
- 2 bay leaves
- 4 celery stalks, washed and finely diced
- 1 tbsp. butter
- 2 apples, cored and coarsely sliced
- 1 tbsp. brown sugar
- 4 oz. Swiss or Jarlsberg cheese, coarsely grated

## Direction

- Preheat the oven to 375°F. Butter a baking pan then place the pork chops. In every chop, insert a clove followed by bay leaves, celery leaves and white wine. Bake in the preheated oven for 30 minutes.
- While the pork chops are baking, sauté diced celery with butter in a frying pan for 5 minutes before adding sliced apples. Scatter brown sugar over the top. For the next 10 minutes, proceed with cooking at an extremely low heat until apples become tender but not mushy. Remove the celery leaves and bay leaves to finish the pork chops. On every chop, scatter cheese. Baste then broil for several minutes until the top is browned.

## 89. Pot Roast In Rich Gravy

*"This pot roast with the flavors of tomato, wine, thyme, bay leaf, and cinnamon is just as good as pot roast in holiday feasts."*
*Serving: Makes 8 servings | Prep: 30m*

## Ingredients

- 1/4 cup matzoh cake meal
- 4 tbsps. vegetable or olive oil, divided
- 1 (4 1/2-to 5-lb.) beef chuck roast, tied
- 1 large onion (about 1 lb.), coarsely chopped (2 cups)
- 2 large carrots (about 1/2 lb.), coarsely chopped
- 2 medium parsnips (about 1/2 lb.), coarsely chopped
- 2 cups full-bodied red wine
- 4 cups chicken broth
- 1 (28-oz.) can diced tomatoes in juice
- 5 full sprigs fresh thyme
- 2 bay leaves
- 1 (3-inch long) cinnamon stick
- Fresh horseradish root, peeled and finely grated for serving (optional)
- a 6- to 7-quart-wide heavy pot with lid

## Direction

- Place the rack in the middle of the oven then preheat to 350 degrees F.
- Combine half tsp. pepper, a tbsp. kosher salt, and matzoh cake meal in a big dish. Pat dry meat and dredge in matzoh mixture; shake the meat off to discard excess mixture. Get rid of the matzoh mixture and keep the dish.
- On medium-high heat, heat 3tbsp oil in a 6-7qt wide and heavy pot until it shimmers. Cook meat for 12mins until all sides are brown; move to a plate.
- Turn to medium heat and put in half tsp. pepper, onions, a tsp. of kosher salt, carrots, and parsnips. Cook and stir from time to time for 8-10mins until the vegetables are golden and soft.

- Pour in wine; boil until it reduces by half while stirring to scrape the bits at the base of the pot.
- Add in cinnamon stick, chicken broth, bay leaves, tomatoes in juice, and thyme; let it simmer. Place the meat in the pot, cover. Put the pot in the oven and braise for three hours until the meat is tender and can be easily pricked with a fork.
- Place meat on a cutting board. Discard the cinnamon stick, bay leaves, and thyme sprigs. Purée two cups of the braising liquid in a blender until smooth. Be careful when blending hot liquids. In the pot with liquid, mix in puréed sauce; tweak seasoning according to taste.
- Remove strings from the meat and slice into thick portions. The tender meat may fall apart while cutting. Place the meat back with the sauce. Serve.
- This dish can be made two days in advance, keep the meat uncut with the sauce. It is easier to cut the meat when cold. Reheat sliced meat in sauce.

## Nutrition Information

- Calories: 414
- Total Carbohydrate: 23 g
- Cholesterol: 99 mg
- Total Fat: 17 g
- Fiber: 5 g
- Protein: 36 g
- Sodium: 328 mg
- Saturated Fat: 5 g

## 90. Prosecco-rose Petal Pops

*"Allow the Prosecco to get flat in the refrigerator before using it, or decant it into a large bowl. And remember to use food-safe rose petals"*
*Serving: Makes 6 pops*

## Ingredients

- 1 cup white grape juice
- 1 cup cold, flat Prosecco
- 1/3 cup rose water
- 1 1/2 tsps. freshly squeezed lemon juice
- About 30 red rosebud petals, rinsed

## Direction

- Combine the Prosecco, lemon and grape juice and rose water in a big bowl and stir well. Pour into ice pop molds until the liquid comes up 1/3 way up. Place a couple of rose petals on top of the liquid and freeze for 30 minutes or until set.
- Remove molds from freezer and repeat the process. Fill them another 1/3 way up and place rose petals. Insert sticks into the molds and place in freezer for another 30 minutes. Remove from freezer and fill the molds all the way up and top with rose petals. Allow to set in freezer for up to one week or a minimum of eight hours.
- Gently run hot water on the outside of molds for several seconds to loosen the pops. Then gently pull the sticks out.

## 91. Punch House Spritz

*"Every household should have its own special spritz – where the ingredients are in stock all the time and the proportions to make it are stored in the mind – and this one is ours. Our spring-summer staple would be an alteration to the classic spritz formula that highlights the Lini's irresistibly fruity Lambrusco Rosato. Gentian-tinged Cocchi Americao provides the bitter aspect while the grapefruit provides the sour and helps with the sweetness and at the same time, it enhances the quality of the Lambrusco. This drink embodies the very philosophy of spritz by being both simple and beautiful. It's typically portioned out in a wine glass or built in a pitcher."*
*Serving: Makes 1 cocktail*

## Ingredients

- 2 oz. Cocchi Americano
- 4 oz. Lini Lambrusco Rosato
- 1 oz. fresh grapefruit juice
- 1 oz. soda water

- 1 grapefruit wheel, for garnish

## Direction

- In a rocks or wine glass with ice, build the ingredients and top with the garnish.

## 92. Quick Cider-mulled Wine

*"Serve this dish as the weather gets more pleasant."*
*Serving: Makes 6 drinks | Prep: 5m*

## Ingredients

- 1 (750 ml) bottle juicy light red wine, such as Beaujolais
- 4 oz. brandy
- 2 cups fresh apple cider
- 2 star anise pods
- 6 whole cloves
- 2 cinnamon sticks; plus 6 more for serving (optional)

## Direction

- Combine brandy, wine, star anise, cloves, apple cider and two cinnamon sticks in a medium pan. Bring to boil then reduce heat and simmer on low heat for 15 minutes or until the flavors are infused.
- Serve in mugs garnished with six cinnamon sticks, if desired.
- You can make mulled wine two hours ahead of serving or it may be chilled for up to three days. Warm over medium heat before being served.

## Nutrition Information

- Calories: 190
- Total Carbohydrate: 13 g
- Total Fat: 0 g
- Fiber: 0 g
- Protein: 0 g
- Sodium: 9 mg
- Saturated Fat: 0 g

## 93. Red Wine And Pear Brioche Tart

*"The uncommon crust made up of brioche dough makes for an interesting dish."*
*Serving: Makes 6 to 8 servings*

## Ingredients

- 1 1/2cups all purpose flour
- 3 tbsps. sugar
- 2 tsps. dry yeast
- 3/4 tsp. salt
- 6 tbsps. chilled unsalted butter, cut into 1/2-inch cubes
- 2 large eggs
- 2 tbsps. whole milk
- 1 3/4 cups dry red wine
- 3/4 cup plus 2 tbsps. sugar
- 1 1/4 lbs. Bosc pears (3 medium), peeled, quartered, cored, each quarter cut into 3 wedges
- 1 tsp. cornstarch
- 1 tsp. water
- crème fraîche or sour cream

## Direction

- To make the brioche crust, begin by buttering a 9-inch springform pan. In a processor, mix salt, yeast, sugar, flour and butter. With the use of the on and off turns, blend until the butter turns into pea-sized pieces then insert the milk and eggs. Blend with the on and off turns until sticky dough forms. Press the dough onto the bottom of the pan with buttered fingertips and cover it up with plastic. Leave the dough to rise for 1-3/4 hours in a draft-free, warm area until it doubles in volume.
- Meanwhile, in a medium saucepan for preparing filling and sauce at medium-high heat, stir 3/4-cup of sugar and wine until the mixture boils and the sugar dissolves before adding the pears. Adjust the heat to medium-low and let it simmer for about 8 minutes until

the pears turn tender. Leave the mixture to cool for 30 minutes.

- Use a slotted spoon to transfer the pears onto a plate. Boil the wine syrup inside of a pan for 4 minutes until it reduces to 1 cup. In a small bowl, mix 1 tsp. of water and corn-starch together before adding it into the wine syrup. Cook for about 1 more minute or until the syrup boils and thickens, whisking from time to time. Set the sauce aside.
- Place the rack on the top third of oven and preheat it to 400°F. Leaving 1/2-inch of plain border on the dough, start arranging pear slices from the edge of the pan in concentric circles close on dough to one another. Sprinkle 2 tbsps. of sugar over the dough edge and pears. Bake the tart for about 30 minutes. It is done when the crust is thoroughly cooked, the pears turn tender and the edges are browned. Move it onto the rack, releasing pan sides. Give it a minimum of 15 minutes to cool down before cutting the tart into wedges. Set on serving plates then serve with crème fraîche and sauce.

## Nutrition Information

- Calories: 486
- Total Carbohydrate: 77 g
- Cholesterol: 93 mg
- Total Fat: 14 g
- Fiber: 4 g
- Protein: 7 g
- Sodium: 322 mg
- Saturated Fat: 8 g

## 94. Red Wine-braised Lamb Shanks

*Serving: Serves 4*

## Ingredients

- 2 tbsps. olive oil
- 4 lamb shanks (about 3 1/2 lbs.)
- 1 large onion, chopped
- 4 large garlic cloves, minced
- 1 28-oz. can ready-cut tomatoes
- 1 1/2 cups dry red wine
- 1 tsp. dried marjoram, crumbled

## Direction

- On medium-high heat, cook oil in a heavy big skillet. Place lamb shanks and fry until color turns brown for about 12 minutes, flipping occasionally.
- Put the lamb into the plate and lower heat to low. Toss in garlic and onion; stir-fry for about 6 minutes until tender. Add the lamb back to the skillet. Put the tomatoes with the juices and pour red wine. Add in marjoram and sprinkle pepper and salt, generously to season. Cover, allow simmering for about 2 hours, flipping occasionally, until lamb shanks tenderized. (Cooked lamb shanks can be done 1 day ahead. Keep in the refrigerator with cover. To use: Boil again before proceeding.) If needed, allow the liquid to boil without cover until the liquid consistency is reduced to the consistency of the sauce.

## Nutrition Information

- Calories: 823
- Total Carbohydrate: 14 g
- Cholesterol: 217 mg
- Total Fat: 52 g
- Fiber: 5 g
- Protein: 64 g
- Sodium: 480 mg
- Saturated Fat: 22 g

## 95. Red Wine-raspberry Sorbet

*"There might only be a few ingredients and it might look like a piece of cake to make, but the outcome is amazing! This is my top choice of sorbet, always."*
*Serving: Makes about 1 quart (1 liter)*

## Ingredients

- 1 cup (200 g) sugar

- 3/4 cup (180 ml) water
- 1 bottle (750 ml) fruity red wine, such as Merlot, Zinfandel, or Beaujolais
- 3 cups (15 oz./400 g) raspberries

## Direction

- Boil and stir red wine, water and sugar in a midsized pan for 1 minute or until the sugar dissolves. Move it away from the heat then insert raspberries and cover it up. For the next hour, leave it steeping. Set a mesh strainer over a midsized bowl. Get a rubber spatula to crush the mixture over the strainer to puree and remove the seeds of the berries. Alternatively, you can put it through a food mill with a fine disk into a medium bowl. Cover the bowl up and keep it in the fridge until it becomes completely chilled. Follow the manufacturer's directions to use the ice cream machine to freeze it up.

## 96. Red-cooked Pork Belly

*Serving: Makes 6 to 8 servings as part of a Chinese dinner | Prep: 40m*

## Ingredients

- 1 1/2 qt water
- 1 (2- to 2 1/2-lb) piece fresh pork belly (unsmoked bacon; about 3 inches thick) with skin and bones
- 1/4 cup Chinese rice wine (preferably Shaoxing) or medium-dry Sherry
- 3 garlic cloves, smashed
- 6 (1/4-inch-thick) slices fresh ginger
- 1 1/2 tbsps. dark soy sauce
- 1 1/2 tbsps. regular soy sauce (sometimes labeled "light" or "thin" soy sauce)
- 1/2 cup coarsely crushed yellow rock sugar (sometimes labeled "yellow rock candy")
- 1 tsp. kosher salt
- 12 baby bok choy (preferably Shanghai; 2 1/2 inches long), halved lengthwise (1 1/2 lb total)
- Accompaniment: cooked rice

## Direction

- In a heavy 3 to 4-quart pot, pour water and bring to boil. Place pork belly, allowing water to boil again. Skim the foam formed then pour wine. Lower heat to moderate and cover partially, allow to simmer briskly, skimming the foam occasionally, for 20 minutes. Toss in the rest of the ingredients excluding bok choy. Lower heat to low and cover partially, allow to simmer while flipping the pork occasionally until meat and skin tenderized for about 3 hours.
- Using tongs and spatula, transfer pork into the platter. Cover using foil to keep pork warm. In a 12-inch heavy skillet, add cooking liquid (don't remove the fat), allow boiling until reduced into about 1 cup syrup for about 25 minutes. Prepare a fine-mesh sieve over a bowl and pour syrup; throw away any solids.
- In a big pot, allow water to boil and add bok choy to cook until crisp-tender and bright green for about 2 minutes. Use a colander to drain thoroughly and using paper towels to pat dry bok choy. Place bok choy around the pork. Pour sauce on top of the meat and drizzle a few on top of the vegetables.
- NOTE: Pork belly can be cooked 3 days ahead and cooled without cover, in unreduced cooking liquid. Keep in the chiller with cover.

## Nutrition Information

- Calories: 985
- Total Carbohydrate: 23 g
- Cholesterol: 122 mg
- Total Fat: 91 g
- Fiber: 2 g
- Protein: 19 g
- Sodium: 832 mg
- Saturated Fat: 33 g

## 97. Rhubarb Shortcakes

*"For a lively hue, choose dark-red stalks. Just remember that the stalks' color, which can range from pale pink to deep red, will influence the filling color."*
*Serving: Makes 8 servings*

### Ingredients

- 2 lbs. rhubarb, trimmed, sliced 1" thick
- 1 cup sugar
- 1/2 cup red wine
- 1 vanilla bean, split lengthwise
- 1 cup cake flour
- 4 tsps. baking powder
- 1 tbsp. sugar
- 1 1/2 tsps. kosher salt
- 1 cup all-purpose flour plus more for work surface
- 3 cups chilled heavy cream, divided
- 1/4 cup (1/2 stick) unsalted butter, melted

### Direction

- For the roasted rhubarb, set the oven to preheat at 350°F. In an ovenproof skillet or medium baking dish, mix the rhubarb, wine, and sugar. Scrape the seeds from the vanilla bean and add it into the mixture. Add the bean and toss the mixture well to combine.
- Roast for 30-40 minutes until the juices are syrupy and the rhubarb is very tender. Take note that the roasting time will depend on the thickness of the stalk. Let it cool. Discard the bean of vanilla.
- For the biscuits and assembly, set the oven to 375°F for preheating. In a medium bowl, mix the sugar, baking powder, a cup of all-purpose flour, salt, and cake flour until well-combined. Add 1 1/2 cups of cream and mix gently until the dough holds together.
- Place the dough into the lightly floured surface. Form it into a rectangle with a size of 9x6" and with a thickness of 1". Cut it into half lengthwise, and then cut it crosswise 3 times until you form 8 rectangular biscuits.
- Line the baking sheet with a parchment paper and arrange the biscuits, positioning them 1" apart from each other. Coat the sides and tops of the biscuits with butter and bake for 18-20 minutes until golden brown. Let them cool in a wire rack. You can serve the biscuits either warm or at room temperature.
- In a medium bowl, whisk 1 1/2 cups of remaining cream until it forms soft peaks. Split the biscuits and brush the cut sides with leftover melted butter. Spread the roasted rhubarb into the biscuits. Serve them together with whipped cream.
- Take note: The rhubarb filling can be prepared 5 days ahead. Just let it cool, cover, and chill. Before serving, reheat the filling slightly. Also, the biscuits can be made a day ahead. Just let it cool completely and store it inside an airtight container. Place it at room temperature.

### Nutrition Information

- Calories: 615
- Total Carbohydrate: 60 g
- Cholesterol: 138 mg
- Total Fat: 39 g
- Fiber: 3 g
- Protein: 6 g
- Sodium: 575 mg
- Saturated Fat: 24 g

## 98. Rhubarb Spritzer

*"To achieve the pretty color for this drink, use rhubarb with no green markings. Do not discard the fibrous pink peel."*
*Serving: Makes 8 servings*

### Ingredients

- 10 oz. rhubarb (about 3 medium stalks), cut into 1/2-inch slices
- 3/4 cup sugar
- 1 tbsp. fresh lemon juice
- 3 cups seltzer or 1 bottle (750 ml) dry sparkling Cava wine, chilled
- Lemon and pink grapefruit slices, halved (optional)

## Direction

- On medium heat, combine lemon juice, rhubarb, and sugar in a medium pot until the sugar is dissolved. Boil then turn to medium-low heat. Let it simmer for 6mins until the rhubarb is completely broken down, stir from time to time. Use a sieve with fine mesh to filter; press the solid down to squeeze as much liquid. Get rid of the solids then cover. Chill until cold or for at least 2hrs to a day.
- Split syrup between eight glasses; add cava or seltzer on top. If desired, add slices of grapefruit and lemon. Serve right away.

## 99. Rib-eye Fajitas On The Grill

*"Planning for a fest? Try this backyard perfect party with do-it-yourself fajita, steal, sour cream and guacamole."*
*Serving: Serves 8 to 12*

## Ingredients

- 3 tbsps. soy sauce
- 3 tbsps. freshly squeezed lime juice (about 1 1/2 medium limes)
- 3 tbsps. Worcestershire sauce
- 6 cloves garlic, crushed
- 1 1/2 cups red wine
- 1/4 cup vegetable oil
- 5 lbs. boneless rib-eye steaks
- 1 poblano chile
- 4 Anaheim chiles
- 8 bell peppers (2 green plus 6 in any assortment of red, yellow, or orange)
- 2 tbsps. freshly squeezed lemon juice (about 1 medium lemon)
- Pinch of kosher salt
- 12 tortillas (flour or corn)
- 2 large yellow onions, cut in 2-inch-thick slices
- Sour cream, for accompaniment
- Guacamole (page 255), for accompaniment
- Beans a la Charra (page 150), for accompaniment

## Direction

- Marinating the meat: To make the marinade, mix the lime juice, wine, vegetable oil, soy sauce, Worcestershire sauce, and garlic into a big measuring cup (4 cups). In a big resealable plastic bag that's heavy-duty, place the steaks and marinade; seal. Keep in refrigerator for at least 4 hours or overnight.
- Heat the outdoor grill to 250 degrees F. Place the bell peppers whole and chiles into the grill; cook until it turns brown in color and blister, use tongs for flipping every few minutes to grill all sides. Take out from heat; seed and core. Slice in lengthwise the grilled chiles and pepper into 1/2 inch strips. Season with a pinch of salt and lemon juice. Using an aluminum foil, wrap the chiles and pepper. Place in the oven to keep it warm until use. Use the foil to wrap the tortillas and place in the oven together with the peppers to keep warm. Drain the marinade from steaks. Roast the steak in your desired doneness. Add the onion slices to grill together with steak for about 5 minutes per side.
- Serving: Slice thinly the steaks. Put the grilled onion slices, peppers, and chiles in a decorative arrangement on a big platter. Place the warm tortillas, bowls of guacamole and sour cream together with the platter. Serve along with Beans à la Charra, in small bowls, is another classic fajita accompaniment
- Alternative: You can use substitute beef to skinless, boneless breasts of chicken or shrimp. Follow the procedure above to marinate the chicken. If using shrimp, exclude the marinade procedure and just massage the shrimp with a pinch of kosher pepper and salt then grill.

## 100. Risotto With Amarone And Caramelized Radicchio

*"Best made with radicchio di Treviso found at many farmers' markets."*
*Serving: 6–8 first-course servings | Prep: 45m*

### Ingredients

- 4 tbsps. (1/2 stick) butter, divided
- 1/4 cup extra-virgin olive oil
- 1 cup minced onion
- 2 large heads of radicchio, halved, cored, cut into 1/3-inch strips
- 2 cups arborio rice or medium-grain white rice (about 13 oz.)
- 1 cup amarone or other dry red wine
- 6 cups (about) low-salt chicken broth
- 1 cup freshly grated Parmesan cheese

### Direction

- Place a big heavy skillet on medium high heat and melt one tbsp. of butter along with the olive oil. Toss in the radicchio and onion and sauté for approximately 18 minutes until they begin to brown. Add in the rice, and season with pepper and salt. Allow rice to cook, until the rice is half cooked, gently stirring all the time. After around three minutes, when the rice seems translucent along the edges but still quite opaque in the centre, add the wine. Allow to simmer for around three minutes until the wine gets absorbed by the rice. Stir occasionally. Increase heat and add 5 1/2 cups broth. When the rice starts boiling, reduce heat and let simmer until the rice is cooked and the risotto looks creamy. Stir occasionally and add more broth if needed. Continue cooking for around 18 minutes. Remove from heat and stir in the parmesan cheese and 3 tbsps. butter. Season to taste with pepper and salt and serve immediately.

### Nutrition Information

- Calories: 491

- Total Carbohydrate: 54 g
- Cholesterol: 34 mg
- Total Fat: 23 g
- Fiber: 2 g
- Protein: 15 g
- Sodium: 286 mg
- Saturated Fat: 9 g

## 101. Roast Cornish Game Hen With Spring Vegetables

*"This dish can be made in just 45mins or less. Combine endive spears with vinegar and oil. Cherry tomatoes are best paired with the orzo pilaf. Crème fraîche with the rhubarb compote is perfect for dessert."*
*Serving: Serves 2; can be doubled*

### Ingredients

- 1 large fresh fennel bulb, trimmed, thinly sliced
- 1 large leek (white and pale green parts only), thinly sliced
- 1 1/2 cups peeled baby carrots
- 2 tsps. dried thyme
- 1 1/2 tbsps. olive oil
- 1 1 1/2-lb. Cornish game hen, halved lengthwise
- 1/2 cup dry white wine

### Direction

- Preheat the oven to 500 degrees F. In a 13-in x 9-in x 2-in glass baking pan, mix a tbsp. oil, fennel, a tsp. thyme, carrots, and leek; mix to cover then season with pepper and salt. Slather the remaining half tbsp. of oil oven hen halves; season with salt, a tsp. thyme, and pepper. Place hen halves over the veggies and roast for 15mins.
- Pour in wine. Keep on roasting for another 8mins until the hen is cooked and the veggies are tender; mix veggies from time to time. Serve hen along with veggies.

## Nutrition Information

- Calories: 648
- Total Carbohydrate: 28 g
- Cholesterol: 210 mg
- Total Fat: 40 g
- Fiber: 9 g
- Protein: 39 g
- Sodium: 287 mg
- Saturated Fat: 10 g

## 102. Roast Rack Of Lamb With Madeira-peppercorn Reduction

*"Serve the lamb with onion and potato gratin with boiled haricots verts, and a salad and wine of your choice. End with a French apple tart topped with some crème fraiche."*
*Serving: 4 servings*

## Ingredients

- 6 medium shallots
- 4 tbsps. (1/2 stick) chilled unsalted butter
- 1 1/4 cups Madeira
- 1 tbsp. drained green peppercorns in brine, coarsely chopped
- 2 1 1/4-lb. racks of lamb, trimmed

## Direction

- Chop two medium shallots finely. In a small heavy pan on medium heat, heat 1 tbsp. butter till it melts. Sauté chopped shallots for a couple of minutes until tender. Add green peppercorns and madeira. Boil for 10-12 minutes, uncovered, until the mixture reduces to one cup. Take sauce off heat.
- Cut and push four medium shallot through a garlic press. Place lamb of rimmed baking sheet and coat with the pressed shallots. Season with pepper and salt. Cover both the lamb and sauce, separately, and allow to cool in refrigerator for up to eight hours if making this ahead of time.
- Roast lamb in preheated oven (400-degree F) for 25 minutes. Increase temperature to 500-

degree F and continue roasting for a further five minutes until the lamb becomes a nice brown colour. When inserted in the middle of the roasted lamb, a meat thermometer should show 130-degree F.
- Simmer the peppercorn sauce and whisk in 3 tbsps. butter. Season to taste with pepper and salt. Before serving, use a sharp carving knife to cut lamb to chops by cutting between the ribs. Serve with peppercorn sauce poured around the chops.

## Nutrition Information

- Calories: 992
- Total Carbohydrate: 21 g
- Cholesterol: 188 mg
- Total Fat: 83 g
- Fiber: 3 g
- Protein: 33 g
- Sodium: 131 mg
- Saturated Fat: 39 g

## 103. Roasted Leg Of Lamb With North African Spices, Lemon, And Onions

*"Spiked with Harissa, this herb and spice rub contains caraway, turmeric, cumin and the classic rosemary and oregano and is great for beef, pork or poultry. Rub the mixture over the meat a couple of hours before grilling. You can even this rub in equal proportions with yogurt and baste meat before grilling. For added flavor, leave the marinated meat overnight in the refrigerator."*
*Serving: 6 servings*

## Ingredients

- 3 tbsps. coarse sea salt
- 2 tsps. dried Greek oregano or savory
- 1 tsp. chopped fresh rosemary leaves
- 3 tsps. caraway seeds
- 1 tsp. cumin seeds
- 1/2 tsp. ground turmeric
- 2 tbsps. Harissa or Aleppo or Mara's pepper to taste

- 1 tsp. chopped garlic
- 1/4 cup olive oil
- One 5-to 6-lb. bone-in leg of lamb
- 1/4 cup fresh lemon juice
- 1/3 cup dry white wine, or more if needed
- 1½ lbs. medium or small red onions, peeled and halved or quartered
- 2 or 3 fresh rosemary sprigs, or 1 tbsp. dried

## Direction

- Finely grind rosemary, cumin, caraway, turmeric, oregano and salt in a coffee or spice grinder. Turn out in a clean bowl and add the chopped garlic and harissa along with the olive oil to get a thick paste. Make several deep slits on the lamb and rub the spice paste in the slits and on the meat. Cover and refrigerate overnight or for five hours. Alternately, let the lamb rest for one hour at room temperature. Before roasting, bring the meat to room temperature.
- Heat an oven to 450 degrees F. Put a lamb leg with the fat side down inside a roasting pan that can hold onions in a single layer. Roast it for 20 minutes. Mix wine and lemon juice in a small bowl. Flip the meat and place the wine-lemon mixture on it. If you are using a clay dish, make the mixture warm first, because the cold liquid can crack the clay. Bring the oven temperature down to 37-degree F then roast it for 35 minutes. Baste it at 10-15-minute intervals using the pan juices. Add extra wine is the pan becomes dry.
- Place lamb on a plate and put onions. Coat by tossing well with pan juices. Place sprigs of rosemary and dash on dried rosemary. Mix. Put lamb on onions and roast again for 30 more minutes while frequently roasting. An instant-read thermometer in the biggest section of meat should say 135-degree F. place meat on a heated platter. Use a double layer aluminium foil to cover it and put it aside. Keep oven on. Put majority of it in a saucepan and briefly cook to reduce if the pan juices are too watery.

- While roasting, place the pan back in the oven and bake until onions become tender and edges that are brown. Place oven on broil. Put lamb on onions and broil them for 2-3 minutes, or until surface is crackling and deep brown. Crave lamb and eat. Place pan juices in a sauceboat or bowl to eat with.

## 104. Rum Fustian

*"Give this interesting spice-filled, alcohol-infused dessert a try."*
*Serving: Makes about 8 drinks. If there is a problem with eggs in your region, do not prepare this recipe.*

### Ingredients

- 6 egg yolks
- 1 quart beer or ale
- 1 pint gin
- 1 pint medium dry sherry
- 1 stick cinnamon
- Dash nutmeg
- Twist lemon peel

### Direction

- Whisk egg yolks until they turn frothy and lemony before beating in the beer and gin. In a saucepan, mix the sherry with lemon peel, nutmeg and cinnamon then heat it up until just boiling. Extract the cinnamon and stir the hot wine together with the egg mixture. Transfer it into heated 8-oz. mugs and serve at once. It's best enjoyed warm.

### Nutrition Information

- Calories: 236
- Total Carbohydrate: 6 g
- Cholesterol: 110 mg
- Total Fat: 3 g
- Fiber: 0 g
- Protein: 2 g
- Sodium: 223 mg
- Saturated Fat: 1 g

## 105. Rump Of Beef To Stew

*"Make this stew a day in advance and relish the flavor!"*
*Serving: Serves 6 to 8*

### Ingredients

- 1 boneless rump roast (3 1/2 to 4 lbs.)
- Water as needed
- 2 tsps. salt
- 1 tsp. ground black pepper
- 1/4 tsp. ground cloves
- 1/2 tsp. ground nutmeg
- 1/2 tsp. ground mace
- 1 tsp. dried marjoram
- 3/4 tsp. dried savory
- 2 tsps. dried thyme
- 2 tbsps. chopped fresh parsley
- 1 large egg yolk, lightly beaten
- 2 cups dry red wine, such as claret or merlot
- 1/2 cup balsamic vinegar
- 1 medium onion, peeled, halved lengthwise, and thinly sliced
- 2 tbsps. unsalted butter
- Peeled boiled new potatoes for serving
- Orange slices for garnish

### Direction

- Rinse, pat dry, and place roast in a Dutch oven with enough water to reach halfway up its sides. Bring to a boil, covered. When it starts boiling reduce the heat and let simmer for an hour. Turn the roast a couple of times to prevent sticking to the bottom of the pan. Remove from pan and keep aside to cool. Save the liquid.
- When the roast is cool enough to handle, use a sharp knife to create several slits at the top. Combine parsley, thyme, savory, marjoram, salt, pepper, mace, cloves and nutmeg in a small bowl. Rub this on the surface and in the slits of the roast. Separately beat an egg yolk and smear over the roast.
- Put roast back in the oven. Add balsamic vinegar and red, stir well with cooking liquid.

Boil on medium high heat, covered. Lower heat and simmer for 1 hour, covered. Add onion and simmer for another hour, covered. Occasionally turn and mix gravy until beef becomes tender enough to pierce with a fork
- Carefully lift the roast from the pan and place on a clean surface. Loosely cover with aluminium foil. Heat the leftover gravy until it begins to simmer. Season with salt and pepper and whisk in the butter. Stir well until gravy becomes smooth.
- Before serving, thinly slice the beef and place on a serving dish. Place boiled potatoes around the beef and pour gravy on the potatoes and the beef. Garnish with slices of orange. Serve the leftover gravy in a sauceboat.

## 106. Sake Kasu-marinated Sea Bass With Coconut Green Curry Sauce

*Serving: Serves 6*

### Ingredients

- a 1-inch piece fresh gingerroot
- 1 cup mirin*
- 1/2 cup sake kasu* (fermented lees of Japanese rice wine)
- 1/2 cup tamari* or soy sauce
- 1/4 cup white miso*
- 1/4 cup rice vinegar (not seasoned)
- 2 tbsps. packed brown sugar
- six 6- to 7-oz. skinless pieces Chilean sea bass fillet (each about 1 1/2 inches thick)
- 1 tbsp. vegetable oil
- Accompaniment: Coconut Green Curry Sauce
- *available at Japanese markets and by mail order from Uwajimaya,tel. (800) 889-1928

### Direction

- Prepare marinade by blending peeled and chopped gingerroot with the rest of the ingredients for the marinade in a blender until smooth.

- Take a shallow dish and place the sea bass in it. Spoon the marinade on the fish and coat well on both sides. Cover and chill for a minimum of two hours.
- Wrap the handle of a medium sized non-stick pan with three layers of foil taking care to keep the shiny side out. Gently lift the fish from the marinade and place it on a platter. Discard the marinade. Heat oil in prepared skillet and sear fish on one side for approximately three minutes until golden brown, on medium high heat. Turn fish over and place skillet in preheated over (400 deg F). Allow fish to roast in oven for about 8 minutes or until well done. Serve hot with curry sauce.

## Nutrition Information

- Calories: 333
- Total Carbohydrate: 12 g
- Cholesterol: 76 mg
- Total Fat: 7 g
- Fiber: 1 g
- Protein: 37 g
- Sodium: 1723 mg
- Saturated Fat: 1 g

---

## 107. Salmon With Black Bean Sauce

*"Fermented black beans are versatile, it works well with any protein and can also be made into a sauce. You can remove extra salty taste by soaking them. This sauce recipe can be paired with stir-fried veggies, salmon, tofu, shrimp, or chicken."*
*Serving: Makes 4 servings*

### Ingredients

- 2 tbsps. fermented black beans, rinsed, drained, and chopped
- Four 6- to 7-oz. skinless pieces center-cut salmon fillet
- 2 tbsps. plus 2 tsps. vegetable oil

- 1 tbsp. finely grated fresh ginger (use a Microplane)
- 1 garlic clove, minced (about 1 tsp.)
- 2/3 cup canned low-sodium chicken broth or Chicken Stock
- 1 1/2 tbsps. rice wine or dry sherry
- 1 tbsp. cornstarch
- 1 tsp. sugar
- 4 scallions, white and green parts, thinly sliced (about 1/2 cup)

### Direction

- Preheat oven to 400 degrees F; oil a shallow roasting pan lightly. In a small bowl, mix chopped beans and a half cup of boiling water. Let it stand for 10mins; drain.
- Place salmon with its skinned-side down on a roasting pan; spread 2tbsp oil over the fish. Bake for 10-12mins until the preferred doneness.
- On medium heat, heat 2tsp oil in a small pot. Cook in garlic, soaked and drained black beans, and ginger for a minute. In a bowl, combine sugar, broth, cornstarch, 1/3 cup water, and wine; pour in the black bean mixture. Boil sauce while mixing regularly and let it simmer for two minutes. Serve salmon with sauce and scallions on top.

---

## 108. Salmon With Mushroom Orzo And Red Wine Sauce

*"Toast the orzo before cooking it to give the pasta a great nutty flavor."*
*Serving: Makes 6 servings*

### Ingredients

- 7 tbsps. olive oil
- 1 large onion, sliced
- 2 cups dry red wine
- 2 cups canned beef broth
- 8 fresh thyme sprigs
- 2 bay leaves
- 1 lb. orzo

- 6 shallots, minced
- 1 lb. mushrooms, sliced
- 5 cups canned low-salt chicken broth
- 1/2 cup whipping cream
- 2 tbsps. chopped fresh tarragon
- 6 5-oz. skinless boneless salmon fillets
- 1/4 cup (1/2 stick) unsalted butter, cut into pieces

## Direction

- In a big, sturdy saucepan, heat 2 tbsps. of oil over medium heat and add onion. Sauté the onion for 5 minutes then add 1 bay leaf, thyme, beef broth and wine. Boil for about 35 minutes until the liquid reduces to 1 cup. Strain the sauce into a small saucepan.
- Preheat the oven to 350°F. Set the orzo down on a rimmed baking sheet and bake for 20 minutes until golden brown. In another big, sturdy saucepan, heat 2 tbsps. of oil over moderately high heat and add shallots. Sauté for 4 minutes then add the mushrooms and sauté for 10 minutes until golden. Stir in 1 bay leaf, chicken broth and orzo and bring it to a boil. Adjust the heat to medium-low and cook without cover for around 20 minutes, stirring regularly. The broth should be absorbed and the orzo should be tender. Insert tarragon and cream and let it simmer for 5 minutes, stirring every now and then. Add pepper and salt to season.
- In a sturdy, big non-stick skillet over moderately high heat, heat 3 tbsps. of oil. Scatter salt and pepper to the salmon before placing it into the skillet. Sauté the salmon just until cooked through, about 3 minutes on each side.
- Bring the sauce down to a simmer and whisk butter into it until just melted then season with pepper. Spoon the orzo onto plates and layer with salmon then serve together with sauce.

## Nutrition Information

- Calories: 995
- Total Carbohydrate: 77 g
- Cholesterol: 120 mg

- Total Fat: 52 g
- Fiber: 6 g
- Protein: 49 g
- Sodium: 469 mg
- Saturated Fat: 16 g

## 109. Sangria Blanco

*"This recipe of citrus sangria has a taste of bittersweet flavor from Suze, a French aperitif."*
*Serving: Makes 16 servings*

### Ingredients

- 2 lemons, thinly sliced
- 1 pink grapefruit, thinly sliced
- 2 cups fresh pink grapefruit juice
- 1 375-ml bottle Dolin blanc or dry vermouth
- 1 1/2 cups Suze Saveur d'Autrefois
- 3/4 cup pisco
- 1/4 cup torn fresh mint leaves
- 2 750-ml bottles chilled Vinho Verde

### Direction

- In a large bowl or pitcher, combine vermouth, pisco, lemon slices, mint, Suze, and grapefruit slices and juice. Let it chill for at least 4 hours, then add Vinho Verde into the mixture prior to serving. Serve the mixture over ice.
- You can make the citrus mixture for 12 hours before serving time. Keep it chilled.

## 110. Sangria II

*"A fun and simple drink, ideal for outdoor events!""*
*Serving: 8 | Prep: 10m | Ready in: 10m*

### Ingredients

- 1 (750 milliliter) bottle red wine
- 1 liter lemon-lime flavored carbonated beverage
- 1 orange
- 2 limes

- 1 cup fresh pineapple - peeled, cored and chopped
- 1 cup cherries, pitted and halved

## Direction

- In a punch bowl, insert the sliced fruit up into bite size pieces. (You may want to slightly crush the citrus fruits to get a little more of the flavor into the punch.)
- Pour in the bottle of red wine then mix the carbonated soda in gradually and slowly. Try the drink as you're pouring, you don't want to over dilute the wine.

## 111. Sauteed Baby Eggplants

*"These eggplants are best eaten with steamed red snapper."*
*Serving: Makes 4 servings*

## Ingredients

- 1 lb. baby eggplants (6), trimmed and halved lengthwise
- 1 tsp. kosher salt
- 2 tbsps. soy sauce
- 2 tbsps. mirin* (Japanese sweet rice wine)
- 1 1/2 tbsps. vegetable oil

## Direction

- Cut eggplants into halves lengthwise, then peel a strip of skin, 1" wide, opposite the cut side. Sprinkle salt on both the sides of the cut eggplants and allow to drain on a rack set over a pan. Rinse, squeeze to drain moisture and pat them dry using paper towels.
- In a small bowl, combine the mirin and soy sauce. Set aside.
- Place a large, heavy bottomed non-stick pan on medium heat and heat oil. Gently lower the eggplants in the hot oil, keeping the peeled sides down, and fry for no more than six minutes, until brown on the underside.
- Flip eggplants over then brush with the mirin-soy mixture. Continue frying for another five minutes or so, until tender. Turn leftover

mirin-soy mixture to pan and continue to cook for another two minutes or until liquid is absorbed by the eggplants. Turn the eggplants a couple of times while cooking to prevent them from burning.

## Nutrition Information

- Calories: 89
- Total Carbohydrate: 7 g
- Total Fat: 5 g
- Fiber: 3 g
- Protein: 2 g
- Sodium: 442 mg
- Saturated Fat: 0 g

## 112. Sauteed Bass Fillets With Mushrooms, Scallions, And Soy

*"This recipe is for an amazing fish dish with rich juices and a nice blend of flavors."*
*Serving: Makes 4 servings | Prep: 25m*

## Ingredients

- 2 bunches scallions (about 10)
- 1/4 cup soy sauce
- 1/3 cupmirin (Japanese sweet rice wine)*
- 1/3 cup water
- 4 (6-oz.) skinless black bass or other white fish fillets (3/4 to 1 inch thick)
- 2 tbsps. vegetable oil
- 1/2 lb mushrooms, trimmed and cut into 1/4-inch-thick slices

## Direction

- Diagonally, slice the parts of the scallions that are pale green and white into 1-1/2 inch pieces. Fill 1/4 cup with scallion greens that are sliced up thinly and keep the rest for some other time. Mix it with water, mirin and soy. Dry the fish up through patting it and use salt to season. Over medium-high heat in a non-stick skillet around 12 inches, heat the oil until it's hot. Make sure it isn't smoking. For 4 minutes, fry the fish until almost thoroughly cooked through and it turns golden. During the cooking process, flip it over one time. Move the fish to a serving plate. Cover it up loosely with foil to maintain its warmth. (During this period, the fish will still be cooking while it sits). In the skillet over a medium-high heat, boil and stir the combination of soy mixture, scallion pieces and mushrooms for 7 to 8 minutes. It is done when the sauce thickens a little and the mushrooms become tender. Pour the accumulated fish juices from the serving dish into the skillet. Leave it boiling for a minute. Over the fish, spoon the sauce. Scatter scallion greens atop.

## Nutrition Information

- Calories: 290
- Total Carbohydrate: 8 g
- Cholesterol: 85 mg
- Total Fat: 10 g
- Fiber: 2 g
- Protein: 38 g
- Sodium: 977 mg
- Saturated Fat: 2 g

## 113. Sautéed Chicken Paillards With Artichoke Hearts

*"The center of the artichoke is its most flavorful and tender portion. It may be a chore to get but it's totally worth it."*
*Serving: Makes 6 servings*

## Ingredients

- 1 lemon, cut in half
- 3 large artichokes
- 6 skinless boneless chicken breast halves
- 1/4 cup all purpose flour
- 3/4 tsp. salt
- 1/2 tsp. freshly ground black pepper
- 3 tbsps. olive oil, divided
- 1/2 cup minced shallots (about 2 large)
- 1/3 cup dry white wine
- 1 cup low-salt chicken broth
- 4 tsps. chopped fresh tarragon plus additional for sprinkling
- 3 tbsps. chilled butter, cut into 1/2-inch cubes

## Direction

- In a big bowl of cold water, squeeze in one lemon half. Cut off the artichoke stem leaving just an inch, work one artichoke at a time. Remove the dark green leaves leaving only the pale green ones. Remove the upper 2/3 of artichoke leaves using a big jagged knife. Rub the other half of lemon on the cut sides or the artichokes. On the outermost heart and stem of the artichoke, cut the green portions with a paring knife. Slice artichoke into four through stem. Scoop out the fuzzy choke with a spoon. Cut the heart thinly and put in a bowl with lemon water. Repeat steps with the left artichokes.
- On two sheets of plastic wrap, put chicken breast and lb. into half- 1/3 thick with a mallet. In a small bowl, combine pepper, salt, and flour; roll chicken breast in flour mixture and shake off the extra. Put coated chicken on a dish.
- On medium-high heat, heat a tbsp. olive oil in a big heavy pan; put in three chicken breasts. Cook for 3mins on each side until cooked through and golden. Move chicken on a separate plate. Pour another tbsp. of oil in the pan and cook the remaining chicken.
- Pour the leftover tbsp. of oil in the same pan; put in shallots. Sauté for a minute until it starts to become soft. Drain the artichokes and add in the pan. Cook for 3mins until it starts to become soft. Pour in wine and let it simmer for a minute until nearly absorbed, stir to scrape the brown bits at the base of the pan. Put in 4tsp tarragon and chicken broth; let it simmer while covered for 5mins until the hearts are tender. Sprinkle pepper and salt to season. Place the chicken breast along with the juices again in the pan; stir to blend. Take off heat. Stir in butter lightly until it melts; move to a plate. Add more tarragon; serve.

## 114. Savory Mushroom And Parmesan Palmiers

*"Make this delicious elephant ears appetizer using puff pastry from the store."*
*Serving: 48 palmiers | Prep: 45m*

## Ingredients

- 1/4 cup olive oil, plus more for brushing
- 1 lb. cremini mushrooms, trimmed and thinly sliced (5 cups)
- 3 large shallots, thinly sliced
- 6 large garlic cloves, chopped
- 2 bay leaves
- 1 sprig rosemary
- 2 sprigs thyme
- 3 sprigs tarragon
- 2/3 cup dry white wine
- 1/4 cup Marsala wine
- 6 tbsps. unsalted butter
- 1/2 cup panko (Japanese breadcrumbs) or plain coarse breadcrumbs
- 1/2 cup grated Parmesan (2 oz.)
- 2 tsps. kosher salt
- 1 1/2 tsps. freshly ground black pepper
- All-purpose flour, for rolling
- 12 oz. all-butter puff pastry, frozen and thawed
- Flaky sea salt, for sprinkling
- Two large rimmed baking sheets; parchment paper

## Direction

- In a big and deep pan, heat oil; add in garlic, shallots, and mushrooms. On medium-high heat, cook and stir frequently for 15mins until they start to brown. Using a kitchen string, bind tarragon, bay leaves, thyme, and rosemary together then put in the pan. Pour in a quarter cup and two tbsp. water, Marsala, and wine. Cook for half an hour until the liquid evaporates, stir from time to time. Take out the bundle of herbs; mix pepper, panko, salt, and Parmesan in the mixture. Puree the mixture on a food processor until smooth; allow the mixture to cool down to room temperature.

- Spread the puff pastry to a rectangle measuring 9-in x 15-in on a floured workspace. Put the rectangle on a rimmed baking sheet lined with parchment paper; freeze for 5mins until firm. Evenly slather mushroom purée over the puff pastry. Firmly roll the pastry from one long side up until the middle. Repeat the motion on the other side. Softly stretch the roll until 18 inches long. Freeze for an hour until firm.

- Preheat the oven to 400 degrees F; position the rack on the upper and lower thirds of the oven. Place parchment paper on another rimmed baking sheet. With a big sharp knife, halve the roll crosswise and slice into quarter-inch portions. Place the slices an inch apart on the baking sheet. Slather oil and add flaky salt. Bake for half an hour until palmiers are crisp and golden, turn the sheets from up to down and back to front after 15mins of cooking time. Allow the ears to cool on baking sheets.

- You can make the logs a week in advance. Wrap them in plastic and freeze. The palmiers can be cooked a week in advance; place in a lidded container and store at room temperature. Crisp them again in a 325 degrees F oven for 8-10mins. Serve.

## Nutrition Information

- Calories: 82
- Total Carbohydrate: 6 g
- Cholesterol: 5 mg
- Total Fat: 6 g
- Fiber: 0 g
- Protein: 2 g
- Sodium: 72 mg
- Saturated Fat: 2 g

## 115. Sea Bass With Watercress Sauce

*"Quick and easy entree for your special weekday dinner. Enjoy!"*
*Serving: Serves 2*

### Ingredients

- 1 tbsp. butter
- 1 tbsp. vegetable oil
- 2 8-oz. sea bass fillets
- 3 tbsps. finely chopped shallots
- 1/4 cup dry Vermouth or dry white wine
- 1/2 cup whipping cream
- 1 cup (packed) chopped trimmed watercress (from 1 bunch, about 6 oz..)

### Direction

- On medium-high heat, add oil and butter into heavy medium skillet; heat until butter melts. Toss in sea bass into the skillet. Cook sea bass just until the middle turns transparent for about 4 minutes per side. Place fish into the plate. Use foil to tent fish and keep warm. Scoop 1 tsp. of drippings from the skillet; discard the rest. Put the shallots in the same skillet and mix for 30 seconds. Pour Vermouth and allow boiling. Let mixture boil continuously for 1 minute. Add the cream and allow the sauce to boil until slightly thick and coats a spoon for about 3 minutes. Pour in the 3/4 cup of watercress into the sauce. Sprinkle pepper and salt to season. Put the fish into the plates. Scoop the sauce around the fish and season with the rest of 1/4 cup of watercress. Serve.

### Nutrition Information

- Calories: 544
- Total Carbohydrate: 5 g
- Cholesterol: 175 mg
- Total Fat: 36 g
- Fiber: 1 g
- Protein: 44 g
- Sodium: 186 mg

- Saturated Fat: 17 g

## 116. Set-it-and-forget-it Roast Pork Shoulder

*"The delicious final dish is worth all the time and effort it takes to prepare this crispy, tender pork shoulder."*
*Serving: 8 servings*

### Ingredients

- 1/4 cup black peppercorns
- 3 tbsps. juniper berries
- 1 tbsps. coriander seeds
- 1/2 cup Diamond Crystal or 1/4 cup plus 1 1/2 tsp. Morton kosher salt
- 3 tbsps. sugar
- 1 (8–10-lb.) skin-on, bone-in pork shoulder (Boston butt)
- 5 sprigs rosemary
- 10 garlic cloves, unpeeled, lightly crushed
- 2 cups dry white wine
- Cranberry sauce, cornichons, and whole grain mustard (for serving)
- A spice mill or mortar and pestle

### Direction

- Prepare a mortar and pestle or a spice mill. Using either one, grind the coriander seeds, juniper berries and peppercorns until they are fine. Move them into a tiny bowl to be combined with sugar and salt.
- Get an X-Acto knife or an extremely sharp paring knife or a box cutter with a 1/3"-blade. Use either one to slice parallel lines into the skin on the pork shoulder. Keep the spacing about 3/4" away from each other.
- Make sure to slice all the way across the fat to get near as possible to the meat without cutting into it. Form a diamond shaped pattern by cutting in between the rows with a pair of kitchen shears, making sure they are 3/4" away from one another. The purpose of slicing until a crosshatch design into the fat is

to allow the spices and salt to seep into the meat and for the insides to be cooked.

- Massage the spice mixture into the whole shoulder and through the cuts in fats, covering any exposed meat Try to get the spices into the fatty layer and not on the surface of the skin, where they may burn as the shoulder roasts. Utilise every single bit of the abundant spices, even though it may seem like a lot Use plastic to cover the shoulder up securely. Leave it chilling for a minimum of 3 hours up to 3 days.
- Preheat the oven to 225°F and put a rack on the lower third section. Use 2 layers of durable foil to generously line a rimmed baking sheet (be generous with the foil unless you really enjoy scrubbing pots and pans after Thanksgiving dinner).
- On the centre of the baking sheet, set the garlic and rosemary sprigs followed by a wire rack atop. Place the pork shoulder down on the rack and move it into the oven. Insert 2 cups of water and wine onto baking sheet and roast the shoulder for a 9 or 10 hours or even through the night. The ideal meat should have a very dark skin and appear to be detaching from bone.
- Without any cover at room temperature, leave the pork shoulder to rest for a minimum of 30 minutes to 5 hours or just until serving time.
- Set the oven in between the range of 350°F to 400°F and heat the roast up again for 5 to 10 minutes before serving. Let the top of the meat warm up and let the fat turn soft, but do not let it turn any more color. Place it with mustard, cornichons and cranberry sauce. Serve the dish warm.

## Nutrition Information

- Calories: 973
- Total Carbohydrate: 10 g
- Cholesterol: 272 mg
- Total Fat: 69 g
- Fiber: 2 g
- Protein: 67 g
- Sodium: 1310 mg

- Saturated Fat: 24 g

## 117.Soba Soup With Spinach And Tofu

*"The Japanese noodle connoisseurs view soba – made almost entirely out of buckwheat flour – in a superior light. In this recipe, the soba noodles are paired with a savoury miso broth. Preparation will only take around or perhaps even less than 45 minutes."*
*Serving: Serves 6*

## Ingredients

- 7 cups water
- a 6-inch length of kombu * (dried kelp), wiped with a dampened cloth
- 1 oz. (about 2 cups) dried bonito flakes*
- 1/2 cup soy sauce
- 3 tbsps. mirin * (syrup rice wine)
- 1 tbsp. sugar
- 1/2 lb. dried soba* (buckwheat noodles)
- 2 carrots, sliced thin
- 1/2 lb. spinach, coarse stems discarded and the leaves washed well, spun dry, and cut crosswise into 1 1/2-inch-wide strips
- 8 to 10 oz. firm tofu (preferably silken), cut into 1/2-inch cubes
- 3 to 4 tbsps. miso* (fermented bean paste), or to taste, if desired
- 2 scallions, minced
- *available at Japanese markets

## Direction

- Boil a saucepan of water together with the kombu. Let the kombu simmer for 2 minutes before extracting it with tongs and discarding. Add the bonito flakes and let the mixture simmer for 3 minutes, stirring from time to time. Stir in the sugar, mirin and soy sauce and let the broth simmer for 5 minutes. Use a fine sieve to strain the broth into a heatproof bowl before pouring it back into the pan.
- Cook the noodles in a kettle of boiling salted water until al dente, about 3 to 5 minutes. Be

careful not to overcook the noodles. Use a colander to drain the noodles then run it through cold water to rinse.

- Insert carrots into the broth and let it simmer with the cover on for 5 minutes. Add the tofu and spinach then let the soup simmer for a minute. In a small bowl, combine the miso and 1/2 cup of soup broth before transferring the mixture back into the pan. Distribute the noodles into 6 big bowls and ladle the soup over each one. Over each serving, sprinkle some scallions.

## Nutrition Information

- Calories: 272
- Total Carbohydrate: 38 g
- Cholesterol: 32 mg
- Total Fat: 6 g
- Fiber: 4 g
- Protein: 16 g
- Sodium: 1613 mg
- Saturated Fat: 1 g

## 118. Sparkling Lemon Cocktail

*"The drink will foam up over the edge of the glass if you pour the bubbly too quickly."*
*Serving: Serves 8*

## Ingredients

- 2 Meyer or regular lemons, thinly sliced into rounds, seeds removed
- 8 sugar cubes
- 1 1/2 tsps. Angostura bitters
- 2 (750-ml) bottles dry Prosecco or other sparkling wine, chilled

## Direction

- Muddle sugar cubes, bitters, and lemons in a big measuring glass until slices of lemon are loosened and sugar is crushed. Divide the mixture between 8 glasses of wine. Fill each glass with Prosecco slowly.

## Nutrition Information

- Calories: 175
- Total Carbohydrate: 10 g
- Total Fat: 0 g
- Fiber: 0 g
- Protein: 0 g
- Sodium: 10 mg
- Saturated Fat: 0 g

## 119. Spiced Hazelnut-pear Cake With Chocolate Sauce

*"Taste the true holiday spirit in every bite of this spiced warm cake full of clove, nutmeg, and cinnamon."*
*Serving: Makes one 9" cake | Prep: 1h15m*

## Ingredients

- 10 ripe but firm Bosc pears (about 3 3/4 lbs.)
- 2 cups dry white wine
- 1/2 cup light brown sugar
- 2 tbsps. unsalted butter, cubed
- 1 tsp. ground cinnamon
- 1 tsp. vanilla extract
- 3/4 cup (1 1/2 sticks) butter, softened, plus more for pan
- 1 cup blanched hazelnuts
- 2 3/4 cups all-purpose flour
- 2 1/4 tsps. baking powder
- 1 1/2 tsps. baking soda
- 1 1/2 tsps. ground cinnamon
- 1/2 tsp. ground cloves
- 1/2 tsp. ground nutmeg
- 1/2 tsp. kosher salt
- 1 1/4 cups light brown sugar
- 1/3 cup granulated sugar
- 3/4 tsp. vanilla extract
- 3 large eggs
- 3 oz. dark chocolate, coarsely chopped
- 1 1/2 cups heavy cream, divided
- A 9" cake pan (preferably springform)

## Direction

- To make poached pears: Peel the pears. Spoon the pears upwards starting from the bottom to 1 1/2 to 2 inch using a small melon baller or 1/2 tsp. measuring spoon to remove the seeds and core. Throw away core and seeds. In a large heavy pot, mix 3 cups of water, butter, pears, cinnamon, wine, vanilla, and brown sugar. Cut parchment into a round to fit inside the pot; cover with pears.
- Allow mixture to boil then lower heat; let mixture simmer while coating the pears with liquid by occasional flipping until very tender but not falling apart for 20 to 25 minutes. Place pears into a big bowl using a slotted spoon. Use the round parchment paper to cover the bowl.
- Boil the poaching liquid. On medium heat, cook until liquid consistency is reduced to syrup thickness for 12-15 minutes (must produce 1/2 cup). Place 5 pears into a medium bowl. Reserve the remaining pears for later. Pour over the syrup. Use parchment paper to cover the bowl and keep in the chiller to cool overnight.
- Baking of cake: Heat oven to 350 degrees F. Prepare cake pan greasing with butter and lining bottom using parchment paper.
- On a rimmed baking sheet, toast the hazelnuts, stirring occasionally until color turns golden brown for 6-8 minutes. While waiting, combine in a medium bowl the cinnamon, baking powder, salt, baking soda, nutmeg, flour, and cloves.
- Using a food processor, pulse 3/4 cup of hazelnuts and a 1/2 cup of dry ingredients until hazelnuts turn into fine flour. Set aside leftover hazelnuts. Place floured hazelnuts into a bowl together with the dry ingredients.
- Clean the bowl of a food processor then place 5 poached pears. Pulse pears until smooth. Scoop 2 cups of the processed pear and put into a small bowl. Throw away the remaining puree.
- Set a stand mixer fitted with the paddle attachment on medium-high speed, whisk granulated sugar, a 3/4 cup of butter, brown sugar, and vanilla until mixture is fluffy and light for 3-5 minutes. Scrape down the mixture in the bowl and beat in eggs one at a time, whisking thoroughly in each addition.
- Put the half of pear puree, whisking on low speed. Pour half of the flour mixture, whisking on low speed to incorporate. Add in the rest of the pear puree and flour mixture; whisk until well combined. Transfer to the prepared pan and smoothen the top. On a rimmed baking sheet, set the pan. Cook the cake, turning the sheet halfway through until center sets and tester poked at the middle comes out clean for about 1 hour and 15 minutes. Place the pan onto a wire rack to cool.
- Assembling of cake: Coat chilled pears by turning into the liquid. Scoop about 1/2 cup of the liquid into a small saucepan. Put in a 3/4 cup of cream and chocolate. On medium-low heat, cook mixture, whisking just until chocolate melts. Mix to blend and pour into a medium bowl. Keep in the chiller, mixing occasionally to prevent chocolate to set, until room temperature for about 10 minutes.
- Take out the cake from the pan. If the cake is domed, use a serrated knife for trimming the top. Turn over the cake to a 12-inch platter. Peel off the parchment. Poke cake all over the top with a toothpick to create holes. Paint the top of the cake with 1/4 cup of chocolate sauce using a pastry brush.
- Meanwhile, cut coarsely the leftover 1/4 toasted hazelnuts. Using a standard mixer with a fitted whisk attachment, beat the leftover 3/4 cup of cream until medium-soft peaks form.
- Add on top of the cake the pears, hazelnuts, and whipped cream. Add chocolate sauce on top of the pears by drizzling. Serve alongside with the leftover chocolate sauce.
- Cake and pears can be done 2 days ahead. Keep in a chiller on a separate container with a cover.
- For hazelnuts with skins, roast then bundle the nuts into a kitchen towel then thoroughly rub to peel off skins.

## Nutrition Information

- Calories: 7917
- Total Carbohydrate: 930 g
- Cholesterol: 1474 mg
- Total Fat: 420 g
- Fiber: 79 g
- Protein: 94 g
- Sodium: 4138 mg
- Saturated Fat: 211 g

## 120. Springtime Sangria

*"A classic, low-calorie, but delicious drink."*
*Serving: Makes 4 drinks*

### Ingredients

- 1 1/2 cups red or white wine
- 3/4 cup orange juice (no pulp)
- 1/3 cup triple sec
- 1/3 cup apricot brandy
- 1/3 cup Sprite
- 1 apple, cored and diced
- 1 cup red or green (or mixed) grapes
- 1/2 small cucumber, peeled, seeded and diced
- 4-5 ice cubes

### Direction

- In a big pitcher, mix all the ingredients together and stir using a wooden spoon. Serve.

## 121. Steamed Scallion Ginger Fish Fillets With Bok Choy

*"You can use any flaky, white fish in this plate-steamed dish. Use a plate with enough rim to contain the marinade but not bigger in diameter than the skillet used to steam. Use a flat steamer basket just like stainless-steel or Asian bamboo steamers to fit the plate over the steamer. If using ramekin, just place it on the base of the water-filled pan then put the plate over the ramekin."*
*Serving: Makes 4 servings*

### Ingredients

- 1/2 cup light soy sauce
- 2 tbsps. sugar
- 1/2 cup Shaohsing rice wine
- 1/2 tsp. five-spice powder
- 2 lbs. sole fillet, cut into 8 pieces
- 1 (1-inch) piece fresh ginger, finely julienned
- 6 tbsps. vegetable oil
- 8 scallions (white and green parts), cut crosswise into 2-inch lengths, then thinly julienned lengthwise
- Stir-Fried Baby Bok Choy

### Direction

- Combine five-spice powder, soy sauce, rice wine, and sugar in a medium bowl.
- Place fish on two rimmed plated; spread julienned ginger and a tbsp. of soy sauce over each piece. Set the leftover sauce aside. Cover the fish and let it chill in the refrigerator for 15mins.
- Place a flat steamer basket on a big pot. On high heat, boil an inch of water in the pot. Turn to low heat and place a plate of fish on the steamer basket; cover and let it steam for four minutes. Take off heat but do not uncover. Let the remaining steam cook the fish through for another minute. Take the plate out gently and keep it warm in the oven. Boil water in the steamer and steam the second plate of fish the same way.

- Meanwhile, on moderate heat, heat vegetable oil in a small pan; keep the oil warm.
- Split fish between four plates and put julienned scallions on top. Drizzle hot oil over the fish then serve with bok choy right away.

## 122. Strawberry White Wine Cooler

*"What a refreshing and chilling drink!"*
*Serving: Makes 4 Cups*

### Ingredients

- 2 cups strawberries (about 1 pint), trimmed
- 1/3 cup sugar
- a 750-ml. bottle Sauvignon Blanc or other dry white wine, chilled

### Direction

- Mix and toss gently sugar and strawberries together in a small bowl. Allow it 10 minutes to stand. Puree wine and strawberry mixture in a blender until it turns into a smooth. Wine cooler may be prepared four hours in advance and chilled.
- Serve wine cooler chilled over ice.

### Nutrition Information

- Calories: 246
- Total Carbohydrate: 28 g
- Total Fat: 0 g
- Fiber: 2 g
- Protein: 1 g
- Sodium: 10 mg
- Saturated Fat: 0 g

## 123. Strisce Alla Chiantigiana

*"'Chiantigiana' is the Tuscan wine used for the sauce and 'Strisce' means strips. All types of long pasta will do the trick for this dish."*
*Serving: Makes 4 servings*

### Ingredients

- 8 oz. pappardelle or 12 oz. spaghetti
- Kosher salt
- 1 tbsp. olive oil plus more for serving
- 1/2 red onion, thinly sliced
- 4 oz. pancetta, cut into 1/4" pieces
- Freshly ground black pepper
- 1 1/2 cups Chianti or other dry red wine
- 1/4 cup low-sodium chicken broth
- 1/2 cup grated Parmesan (about 2 oz.) plus more, shaved, for serving

### Direction

- In a big pot of salted boiling water, cook and stir the pasta until just al dente, stirring occasionally. Drain the pasta, keeping 1/2-cup of the cooking liquid.
- Meanwhile, in a large skillet over medium heat, heat 1 tbsp. of oil before adding the pancetta and onion. Cook and stir occasionally for about 5 minutes until pancetta turns crisp and brown. Add salt and pepper to season.
- Pour the broth and wine in then bring it to a boil. Cook for 8 to 10 minutes until it the wine is reduced by half, stirring from time to time. Mix 1/2 cup of grated Parmesan cheese, 1/2 cup of reserved cooking liquid and pasta. Cook the pasta for 3 minutes until the pasta is coated with sauce, tossing frequently. Sprinkle with salt and pepper to season. Drizzle oil over the pasta. Before serving, scatter shaved Parmesan over the top.

### Nutrition Information

- Calories: 415
- Total Carbohydrate: 46 g
- Cholesterol: 19 mg
- Total Fat: 16 g

- Fiber: 2 g
- Protein: 12 g
- Sodium: 406 mg
- Saturated Fat: 4 g

## 124. Summer-berry Basil Kissel

*"This dish based on the classic Russian kissel that is made from thick fruit purée made creamy with potato starch. This recipe makes use of cornstarch for a thicker consistency and berries."*

*Serving: Makes 6 servings*

### Ingredients

- 1 vanilla bean
- 1/2 cup sugar
- 3 tbsps. cornstarch
- 1/4 tsp. salt
- 2 cups sweet Muscat such as Val d'Orbieu St.-Jean-de-Minervois
- 5 cups picked-over blackberries
- 4 cups picked-over raspberries
- 1 1/4 cups packed fresh basil sprigs
- 1/2 tsp. fresh lemon juice, or to taste
- Accompaniment: crème fraîche or sour cream

### Direction

- Cut the vanilla bean along the length and scour seeds on a bowl; keep the pod. Stir in salt, cornstarch, and sugar until well blended.
- Simmer 1/8 cup of each berry type and Muscat for two minutes in a pot. Strain mixture in a sieve on a bowl, keep the liquid. In a big bowl, place cooked berries and mix in left fresh berries. Chop the basil coarsely.
- Slowly stir in reserved hot liquid with the sugar mixture until velvety. Move the mixture on a pan and fold in basil. Boil mixture while stirring then let it simmer while stirring for 3mins. Sieve the mixture over the berries right away and mix until well combined, remove basil. Mix in lemon juice. Split kissel between six bowls. Refrigerate while covered for at least two hours to two days.

- Serve dessert with sour cream or crème fraîche.

## Nutrition Information

- Calories: 243
- Total Carbohydrate: 46 g
- Total Fat: 1 g
- Fiber: 12 g
- Protein: 3 g
- Sodium: 100 mg
- Saturated Fat: 0 g

## 125. Super-concentrated Cantonese Chicken Stock

### Ingredients

- 1 lb. chicken breasts
- 1 lb. chicken wings
- 4 cups cold water
- 2 slices of unpeeled fresh ginger (1/4 inch thick each)
- 1 stalk scallion, cut into 1-inch pieces
- 2 tsps. Chinese cooking wine or sherry
- 1 (1/4-oz.) packet unflavored gelatin
- 1/4 cup cold water

### Direction

- On running cold water, rinse the chicken. Transfer chicken in a big pot; pour water until chicken is barely covered. Note: DO NOT use hot water to make the boiling process faster. Using hot tap waters gives cloudy, technically "yucky" and distinct artificial flavor.
- Add the scallions, rice wine, and ginger. On high heat, allow boiling; skim off occasionally the gunky foam formed at the top. This is to get rid of the impurities on the stock that will taint the stock and you.
- Cover leaving a small gap and lower the heat. For 2 hours, let the stock simmer. Take out from the heat. Pour the stock into a fine mesh

strainer or chinois with a big enough container or bowl below.

- Alternative process if the stock does not have enough body to your preference: In another bowl, combine unflavored gelatin and cold water. Add in the chicken stock; whisk.
- For a sweet and deep savory flavor, do not season the stock.
- For storing: Let cool without cover the stock until close to room temperature or lukewarm. Keep in freezer or refrigerator.

## Nutrition Information

- Calories: 34
- Total Carbohydrate: 0 g
- Cholesterol: 16 mg
- Total Fat: 2 g
- Fiber: 0 g
- Protein: 4 g
- Sodium: 32 mg
- Saturated Fat: 1 g

## 126. Sweet Wine Fritters

*Serving: Makes about 3 dozen*

## Ingredients

- 3/4 cup all purpose flour
- 3 tbsps. unsalted butter, melted
- 1 tbsp. beaten egg
- 1 tbsp. sweet white wine
- 1/2 tsp. vanilla extract
- Pinch of salt
- Vegetable oil
- Powdered sugar

## Direction

- In a big bowl, combine the first 6 ingredients to form dough; knead for about 5 minutes until smooth. Mold the dough to balls and using a disk to flatten balls. Wrap using plastic and put on the side for 10 minutes.

- Divide the dough into half. Flour lightly the working surface and scant into 1/8-inch thickness by rolling out one disk. Slice the dough into 1/2 by 6-inch strips. Do again the rolling and cutting with the rest of the dough.
- In a medium, 1 1/2 inch deep saucepan, add in oil. Cook oil at 350 degrees F. Fry cookies in batches of 4 until golden. Place into paper towels using the slotted spoon then drain. Sieve sugar on top of the cookies (Can be done 2 days ahead. Put in a sealed container in room temperature).

## Nutrition Information

- Calories: 173
- Total Carbohydrate: 19 g
- Cholesterol: 24 mg
- Total Fat: 9 g
- Fiber: 1 g
- Protein: 3 g
- Sodium: 75 mg
- Saturated Fat: 6 g

## 127. Tamarind Mango Sangria

*Serving: Makes 10 to 12 drinks | Prep: 15m*

## Ingredients

- 3/4 cup thawed frozen unsweetened tamarind purée
- 2 cups water
- 3/4 cup sugar, or to taste
- 2 1/2 cups diced fresh mangoes (from 2 large)
- 1 (750-ml) bottle chilled dry white wine
- 1/3 cup tequila (preferably reposado)
- 1 cup halved green and red seedless grapes

## Direction

- In a blender, purée 1 1/2 cup mangoes, tamarind, sugar, and water until smooth. Filter through a sieve with medium mesh on a pitcher. Mix in the remaining cup of mangoes, wine, grapes, and tequila; cover. Refrigerate up to a day until ready to serve with ice.

## Nutrition Information

- Calories: 194
- Total Carbohydrate: 32 g
- Total Fat: 0 g
- Fiber: 1 g
- Protein: 1 g
- Sodium: 17 mg
- Saturated Fat: 0 g

## 128. The New York Sour

*Serving: Makes 1 serving*

## Ingredients

- 2 oz. rye or bourbon whiskey
- 1 oz. fresh lemon juice
- 1 oz. simple syrup
- 1/2 oz. fruity red wine (such as Shiraz or Malbec)

## Direction

- In a cocktail shaker, combine one oz. of simple syrup and fresh lemon juice along with two oz. of either bourbon whiskey or rye. Fill the shaker with ice and shake for about half a minute. Strain liquid and pour on ice in a rocks glass. Hold a spoon over the surface of the drink, gently pour half an oz. of fruity red wine like Malbec or Shiraz on the back of the spoon. This will ensure the wine floats on the top of the drink.

## Nutrition Information

- Calories: 236
- Total Carbohydrate: 23 g
- Total Fat: 0 g
- Fiber: 0 g
- Protein: 0 g
- Sodium: 17 mg
- Saturated Fat: 0 g

## 129. Thick White Noodles In Soup, Topped With Eggs And Scallions

*Serving: Makes 4 servings*

## Ingredients

- 1 quart Sanuki Sea Stock
- 2 tbsps. light-colored soy sauce (usukuchi shoyu; see Tips, below)
- 2 tbsps. syrupy rice wine (mirin; see Tips, below)
- pinch of salt, optional
- 1 recipe fresh udon noodles or 8 to 10 oz. dried or semidried udon noodles , cooked (reserve cooking water)
- 4 large eggs, lightly beaten
- 2 scallions, trimmed and finely chopped (white and green portions)
- 1 small knob fresh ginger, peeled and grated to yield about 2 tsps.; optional

## Direction

- Combine rice wine, stock and soy sauce and heat in a medium saucepan until bubbles begin to appear along the outside edges of the soup. Taste and season to taste with salt.
- Spoon boiling hot water from the pan in which the noodles were cooked into warmed bowls, half filling each bowl. Cover the bowls to retain the heat with a flat plate.
- Place the previously cooked noodles in a deep conical strainer and reheat by dipping them back into the boiling water a couple of times. Swirl them around in the strainer to separate them. Lift strainer and tap to remove any excess water. Alternately you may place the cooked noodles into a pot of hot water, swirl them and strain in a colander.
- Turn the noodles into the bowls.
- Beat eggs in a bowl and keep aside. Heat the previously prepared soup until steaming hot. Stir the soup vigorously in one direction. Pour the beaten eggs in a stream and stir the soup in the opposite direction. Turn off the heat.

- Pour the egg drop soup over the noodles and serve immediately, garnished with chopped scallions and grated ginger.

## Nutrition Information

- Calories: 190
- Total Carbohydrate: 13 g
- Cholesterol: 193 mg
- Total Fat: 8 g
- Fiber: 0 g
- Protein: 14 g
- Sodium: 855 mg
- Saturated Fat: 2 g

## 130. Three Dipping Sauces

*"The dressing in this is versatile and great. It's easy to make but works for a variety of dishes from meats to greens. Prepare once, and use it in multiple ways!"*

## Ingredients

- 50 ml (3 tbsps. plus 1 tsp.) peanut oil
- 2 dried chillies
- 3 spring onions (scallions), white part, with 2 cm (3/4-inch) of green left on, finely sliced
- 1 large knob ginger, finely diced
- 2 cloves garlic
- 15 ml (1 tbsp.) shaohsing wine
- 15 ml (1 tbsp.) rice-wine vinegar
- 2 tbsps. sea salt
- 2 tbsps. superfine sugar
- 100 ml (1/2 cup) Chinese black rice vinegar
- 2 large knobs ginger, finely diced
- 30 ml (2 tbsps.) peanut oil
- 4 spring onions (scallions), sliced into rounds
- 2 large knobs ginger, finely diced
- 3 cloves garlic, finely diced
- 2 red chillies, sliced
- 60 ml (1/4 cup) bean paste
- 60 ml (1/4 cup) shaohsing wine
- 60 ml (1/4 cup) rice-wine vinegar
- 4 tbsps. (1/4 cup) crushed yellow rock (or light brown) sugar

## Direction

- For ginger and shallot oil. In a wok, pour in the peanut oil and heat before adding the chillies. Fry until they turn black then throw them away. Give it some time for the oil to cool. Using a mortar and pestle, insert all other ingredients and lightly squash them. Once the oil has cooled, mix it well into the mortar properly. Let it sit for a moment so the flavors can mash together.
- Very good on boiled and fried dishes, and a great dressing for grilled scallop salad.
- For black vinegar and ginger sauce: An hour before serving, allow the mixture of vinegar and diced ginger to stand. You'll find this easy to make but very effective on boiled meats.
- For bean paste sauce: Heat the peanut oil up in a wok to sauté the chillies, garlic, ginger and spring onions. Do this for 3 minutes before inserting the rest of the ingredients and halving the sauce. Move it away from the heat and allow it to cool. If desired, it can be enjoyed warm mixed into steamed vegetables or as a cold dipping sauce.

## Nutrition Information

- Calories: 223
- Total Carbohydrate: 22 g
- Total Fat: 13 g
- Fiber: 2 g
- Protein: 3 g
- Sodium: 444 mg
- Saturated Fat: 2 g

## 131. Turnip Cake (law Bock Gow)

*"It's a delicious and savory cake that is served throughout the year in dim sum homes and most especially on New Year's Day as a sign of wealth and increasing fortunes. Turnip cake is produced from Chinese turnip, law bock, which is a sort of daikon radish. There is also a daikon radish called Japanese daikon radish, which in appearance is comparable to the Chinese turnip. Some product vendors don't know that there's a difference between Chinese turnip and Japanese daikon. The Chinese turnip looks more blemished than the Japanese daikon, which has a creamier white color. Although Chinese turnip is best for this recipe, whatever you use, choose a strong heavy vegetable. Ideally, the turnip should be 8-12-inches long and 4-inches wide. I discard the layer of the Chinese bacon fat under the rind. In a recipe that requires slicing of Chinese bacon, all that is needed is the knife or cleaver of a sturdy cook. However, when the bacon needs to be finely sliced, as in this recipe, the bacon should first be cooked to create it simpler. Make sure you use rice flour and not the glutinous rice flour. This cake can be wrapped in a plastic wrap and stored inside the fridge for 10 days."*

*Serving: Makes one 8-inch cake, about 48 slices*

## Ingredients

- 6 oz. Chinese bacon (lop yok), store bought or homemade
- 1 large Chinese white turnip, about 2 lbs.
- 8 Chinese dried mushrooms
- 1/2 cup Chinese dried shrimp, about 1 1/4 oz.
- 2 tsps. Shao Hsing rice cooking wine
- 1 tsp. sugar
- 2 cups rice flour

## Direction

- Cut the bacon into 3 equal pieces. Arrange them in a 9-inches shallow heatproof bowl. Boil water over high heat in a covered steamer big enough to fit the bowl without touching the steamer's sides. Place the bowl into the steamer carefully. Cover it and adjust the heat to medium. Steam for 15-20 minutes until the juices are visible in the dish and the bacon is softened. You need to check the water level from time to time and refill with boiling water if needed. Remove the dish from the steamer carefully; set aside to cool.
- Peel the turnip carefully and grate to make 4 1/2 cups. Mix the grated turnip in a 3-quart saucepan together with 1-quart of cold water. Let it boil over high heat. Adjust the heat to low. Cover the pan and simmer for 30 minutes until very tender. Let it drain and reserve the cooking liquid used.
- Soak the mushrooms in a medium bowl with a 1/2-cup of cold water for 30 minutes until softened. Drain and squeeze dry, reserving the soaking liquid. Cut and discard the stems. Mince the caps. Soak the dried shrimp in a small bowl with a 1/2 cup of cold water for 30 minutes until softened. Let it drain, reserving the soaking liquid. Chop the shrimp finely, and then set aside.
- Get the bacon from its dish, reserving its juices. Cut it off and discard the rind and the dense fat layer. Slice the remaining meat into paper-thin slices and chop it finely. Stir-fry the chopped bacon in a 14-inches flat-bottomed wok or skillet for 2-3 minutes over medium heat until the meat starts to brown and when it releases fat. Add the shrimp and minced mushrooms. Stir-fry for 2-3 minutes. Add the pan juices from the bacon, sugar, and rice wine. Stir well to combine and remove it from the heat.
- Bring the cooked and drained turnip back into the saucepan. Add the bacon and mushroom mixture, stirring well to combine. Mix the reserved mushroom and shrimp soaking liquids in a large bowl together with the rice flour until smooth. Mix in a cup of hot turnip broth. Transfer this batter into the saucepan. Add the salt and mix well until combined and its consistency is like that of a rice pudding. Transfer the mixture into a heatproof 3-4-inches deep, straight-sided bowl with a size of 8-inches round (like a soufflé dish).
- Boil water over high heat in a covered steamer big enough to fit the dish without touching the steamer's sides. Place the dish into the steamer. Cover it and adjust the heat to medium-low. Steam for 60 minutes until the

cake is firm to touch and all set. You need to check the water level and refill with boiling water if needed. Carefully remove the dish from the steamer and transfer it into a rack. Allow it to cool for 1 hour. Cover and store inside the refrigerator for at least 3-4 hours.

- Using a knife, loosen the sides of the cake. Position the cake rack over the bowl and invert to unmold. Flip the cake onto the cutting board, right-side up. Use plastic to wrap the cake and refrigerate until ready to use.

- Before serving, cut the cake into quarters. Cut each quarter crosswise, about two 2-inches wide strips (not in wedges). Slice each strip crosswise to form scant with 1/2-inch thick. It's a Chinese way of slicing a cake.

- Place the 14-inches flat-bottomed wok or skillet over medium heat and heat until hot, not smoking. Coat the wok with enough oil. Cook the turnip cake slices in batches, about 2-3 minutes per side until they're all golden brown. Serve it together with oyster sauce.

## Nutrition Information

- Calories: 47
- Total Carbohydrate: 7 g
- Cholesterol: 6 mg
- Total Fat: 2 g
- Fiber: 1 g
- Protein: 1 g
- Sodium: 45 mg
- Saturated Fat: 1 g

## 132. Tuscan Porterhouse Steak With Red Wine-peppercorn Jus

*"If you're looking for the ideal steak for two to share, go for a porterhouse. The dry aged – though more costly – yields tastier and tenderer meat. This steak is pan-roasted with thyme, rosemary and Tuscan stalwarts of garlic then served with a smooth red wine reduction."*
*Serving: Makes 2 servings | Prep: 20m*

### Ingredients

- 1 (1 1/2-lb.) porterhouse steak (1- to 1 1/4-inches thick)
- 2 tsps. black peppercorns, coarsely crushed (see Cooks' Notes)
- 2 tsps. kosher salt
- 1 tbsp. vegetable oil
- 3 tbsps. unsalted butter, cut into tbsp. pieces, divided
- 3 garlic cloves, crushed
- 2 (4-inch) sprigs fresh rosemary
- 5 sprigs fresh thyme
- 1/2 cup medium-bodied dry red wine (such as Chianti, Rioja, or merlot)
- 1 cup low-sodium chicken broth
- ovenproof 12-inch heavy skillet

### Direction

- For 15 minutes, leave the steak to stand at room temperature. As that's happening, preheat the oven to 450°F and pat the steak dry. Rub kosher salt and peppercorns on both sides of the steak to season it.

- In a skillet over medium heat, heat 1 tbsp. of butter and oil until butter melts then add the garlic, thyme and rosemary. Over medium heat, cook and stir for 1 minute until the garlic and herbs turn fragrant by stirring occasionally. Insert the steak and cook for 3 minutes on each side until nicely browned. Move the skillet into an oven and cook. Leave it for 5 minutes to get medium-rare meat, which should register on an instant read thermometer at 110°F. For medium doneness, cook for 10 minutes until the thermometer registers at 120°F.

- Use tongs to move the steak to a small platter, reserving the skillet. Let the steak sit for 10 minutes. As the steak is resting, get rid of the oil from the skillet but keep the herbs and garlic inside of it. Over moderately high heat, add wine into the skillet and let it boil for around 2 minutes or until it reduces by half. During the process, scrape up the browned bits. Pour the chicken broth, along with any of the meat juices on the platter, into the skillet and let it boil until it reduces by half, about 5 to 6 minutes. Stir in the remaining 2 tbsps. of butter until well mixed. Add salt to season and keep it warm.
- To carve: Move the steak onto a cutting board. Cut the meat from the bone into two solid pieces of steak. Cut every piece into thin slices then rearrange them around the bone on a platter. Finish off by drizzling with the jus.
- Cooks' Notes: •Coarsely crush the peppercorns with a mortar and pestle or put the peppercorns in a sealable plastic bag and coarsely crush them with the bottom of a heavy skillet, meat pounder or rolling pin.

## Nutrition Information

- Calories: 636
- Total Carbohydrate: 9 g
- Cholesterol: 174 mg
- Total Fat: 40 g
- Fiber: 3 g
- Protein: 53 g
- Sodium: 1268 mg
- Saturated Fat: 17 g

---

### 133. Vanilla Cream And Apricot Tart

*Serving: Serves 8 to 10*

## Ingredients

- 1/2 vanilla bean, cut into 1/2-inch pieces
- 1/2 cup sugar
- 8 oz. cream cheese, room temperature
- 1 tbsp. whipping cream
- 1 tbsp. sour cream
- 2 tbsps. plus 4 tsps. sweet Marsala wine
- 1 All Ready Pie Crust (1/2 15-oz. package), room temperature
- 1/2 cup apricot preserves
- 2 lbs. apricots, pitted, thinly sliced

## Direction

- Use a processor to chop coarsely the vanilla bean. Add in the sugar; process until vanilla bean become finely ground. Sieve sugar using a strainer to remove any large pieces of vanilla bean. Add in the processor the cream cheese, 2 tbsps. Marsala, sugar, sour cream, and cream; blend until smooth. Keep in refrigerator and start preparing the crust.
- Heat oven to 450 degrees F. Flour lightly the working surface and roll out the crust into 13-inch diameter circle. Place the crust into an 11-inch diameter tart pan with a detachable bottom. Using a fork, pierce the crust all over. Put in oven to bake until turns golden for about 16 minutes. Transfer on a rack to completely cool.
- On medium heat, mix the leftover 4 tsps. Marsala and preserves in a heavy small saucepan until preserves dissolve. Paint the crust thinly with some of the preserves. Pour over the cream cheese mixture and add on top the apricots. Paint the apricots with the rest of the preserves. Keep in the refrigerator for at least 1 hour. (Can be done 6 hours ahead)

## Nutrition Information

- Calories: 381
- Total Carbohydrate: 53 g
- Cholesterol: 34 mg
- Total Fat: 18 g
- Fiber: 3 g
- Protein: 4 g
- Sodium: 223 mg
- Saturated Fat: 9 g

## 134. Veal Osso Buco

*"Italy is famous for this classic Milanese dish. Cooked in rich broth of wine and tomato, the meat is salted before cooking to tenderize it."*

### Ingredients

- Four 12-oz. veal shanks
- Kosher salt
- Freshly ground black pepper
- 1 cup vegetable oil
- 1 cup all-purpose flour
- 2 carrots, peeled and diced
- 2 celery ribs, diced
- 1 yellow onion, diced
- 6 garlic cloves, sliced
- 1 cup dry red wine
- 4 cups veal stock or chicken stock
- 3 cups chicken stock
- 3 cups canned plum tomatoes, drained and crushed
- 2 sprigs fresh thyme
- 1 sprig fresh rosemary
- 1 bay leaf
- 1 tbsp. grated fresh horseradish (see Note)
- 2 tbsps. grated lemon zest
- 2 tbsps. chopped fresh flat-leaf parsley

### Direction

- Take a shallow baking dish and place the veal shanks. Sprinkle salt liberally on both the sides. Place in refrigerator to cool for two hours.
- Rinse the shanks and pat them dry using paper towels. To hold the meat and bone together, wrap each shank once around the circumference and secure the twine with a firm knot. Season shanks with pepper.
- Heat oven to 350-degree F.
- Place a big glass dish on high heat. Pour in the oil and let it heat.
- Get a shallow bowl and put flour in it. Dredge shanks in flour and shake off the excess. Cook in hot oil for five minutes for each side or until browned on all sides. Transfer to a platter and put aside. Discard oil if it turns dark and heat up a cup of fresh oil.
- Reduce heat to medium high and toss in the onion, carrots, celery and garlic. Stir for a couple of minutes, then add wine. Boil and allow to cook for a couple of minutes until the liquid reduces to half.
- Add the tomatoes, rosemary, thyme, bay leaf and stocks to the pan along with the veal shanks. Increase heat to high and boil. Transfer casserole to oven and cook for 2 1/2 hours until meat is tender and falls off the bones.
- Discard herbs from the pan. When the shanks come to room temperature, remove from pan and keep aside. Strain liquid into a big pan and allow to come to a boil on medium high heat. Reduce heat. Allow liquid to simmer until it reduces by a quarter, then skim all visible foam or grease. Transfer strained vegetables to the pan and season to taste.
- Before serving remove twine. Place a single veal shank in a serving bowl and spoon vegetables and about 3/4 cup sauce over it. If required, heat the meat and the sauce for ten minutes on low heat, before serving.
- Garnish each veal shank (osso buco) lemon zest, chopped parsley and fresh horseradish. Season with pepper. Alternately you may use prepared horseradish.

### Nutrition Information

- Calories: 308
- Total Carbohydrate: 14 g
- Cholesterol: 53 mg
- Total Fat: 19 g
- Fiber: 2 g
- Protein: 18 g
- Sodium: 729 mg
- Saturated Fat: 2 g

## 135. Veal Scallops Oporto

*Serving: Serves 4*

### Ingredients

- 8 large or 12 medium veal scallops, pounded thin
- Flour
- 6 tbsps. butter
- 3 tbsps. olive oil
- 2/3 cup port
- 1/2 cup heavy cream

### Direction

- Lightly dredge scallops in flour and sauté in olive oil and butter turning occasionally until evenly browned. When the scallops are brown and tender, add port. Allow to cook gently for a couple of minutes and season to taste. Transfer the scallops to a warmed platter. Add cream to pan, stirring to scrape up the brown bits. Thicken with a little beurre manie. Season liquid to taste and pour on the scallops. Serve hot with noodles and a white Burgundy.

### Nutrition Information

- Calories: 393
- Total Carbohydrate: 5 g
- Cholesterol: 93 mg
- Total Fat: 39 g
- Fiber: 0 g
- Protein: 4 g
- Sodium: 113 mg
- Saturated Fat: 19 g

## 136. Venison With Mushroom-wine Sauce

*"A combination of wine, tomato, and mushrooms is the perfect partner for your meaty meal. Add this recipe to your favorites now!"*
*Serving: Serves 4 people*

### Ingredients

- 1/3 cup all-purpose flour
- 1/4 tsp. salt, plus more to taste
- 1/4 tsp. freshly ground black pepper, plus more to taste
- 1 to 1 1/2 lbs. boneless venison steak, cut into 1/2-inch-thick slices
- 1 tbsp. olive oil
- 1/4 cup chopped shallots
- 1 garlic clove, minced
- 1 1/2 cups chopped mushrooms
- 1 tbsp. tomato paste
- 1/2 cup red wine
- 1/2 cup low-sodium chicken broth

### Direction

- In a shallow dish, combine pepper, flour, and salt. Place meat into the seasoned flour to dredge. On medium-high heat, cook oil in a big skillet. For 2 minutes a side, cook venison. Transfer into the plate. Keep venison warm by covering.
- Lower heat in the skillet to medium. Toss in garlic and shallots to cook, constantly stir for 1 minute. Toss in mushroom and stir-fry, about 3 minutes. Add in tomato paste; stir. Pour chicken broth and wine, raising heat to medium-high to cook for another 1 minute. Add again the meat into the pan, allow simmering until meat is heated for about 1 minute. Sprinkle with pepper and salt to taste.

## 137. Vin Santo Zabaglione With Orange And Grapefruit

*"This dish is typically made with egg yolks but in this altered version, just the egg is used and the typical Masala is replaced by vin santo. It ends up being less fattening."*
*Serving: Makes 4 servings | Prep: 20m*

### Ingredients

- 3 medium navel oranges
- 1 large pink or red grapefruit
- 3 tbsps. sugar
- 1 large egg
- 3 tbsps. vin santo or other sweet dessert wine
- 3/4 tsp. cream of tartar
- Garnish: freshly ground nutmeg

### Direction

- Use a sharp knife to get rid of the white pith and peel from the grapefruit and oranges. From the membranes, slice sections of the fruit off. Place a big sieve set over a bowl. Place the fruit on it to leave it draining for 5 minutes. Keep the juice for a different use. Mix 1 tbsp. of sugar with the fruit.
- Over a pot of simmering water inside of a metal bowl set or a double boiler, insert a pinch of salt, cream of tartar, vin santo, remaining 2 tbsps. sugar and egg. At a moderate speed, use a hand-held electric mixer to beat for around 5 minutes until it turns frothy and thickens slightly. Before it thickens, the mixture with froth up and lessen first. Move it away from the heat. Prepared 4-stemmed glasses and distribute the fruit equally into each one. Place the zabaglione atop. Serve immediately.

## 138. Walnut Cheesecakes With Tokay Syrup

*"Scrumptious cheesecake recipe."*
*Serving: Makes 6 servings | Prep: 30m*

### Ingredients

- 1/3 cup Grape Nuts cereal
- 3 tbsps. chopped walnuts, toasted
- 2 pitted dates
- 1/2 tsp. finely grated fresh lemon zest
- 1/8 tsp. cinnamon
- 1 cup 1% cottage cheese
- 4 oz reduced-fat cream cheese
- 2 tbsps. sugar
- 1 large egg white
- 1 tbsp. cornstarch
- 1 tsp. finely grated fresh lemon zest
- 1/2 tsp. vanilla
- 3 tbsps. sugar
- 1/3 cup water
- 2 tbsps. Tokay or Sauternes

### Direction

- Preheat the oven to 300 degrees F.
- Prepare crust. In a food processor, combine crust ingredients until moist and crumbly.
- Grease six 1/3-cup muffin tins and place wax or parchment papers at the bottom. Split crust mixture between muffin tins and push firmly to even it out on the base.
- Prepare the filling and cake. In a food processor, cream cottage cheese until smooth; scuff down the sides of the bowl regularly. Blend in the remaining filling ingredients until smooth. Scoop mixture on muffin cups then place in a hot water bath. Bake in the middle of the oven for 20-25mins until firm. Take it out of the pan and let the pan cool down on a rack. Refrigerate while covered for two hours.
- Meanwhile, boil water and sugar in a small pot on high heat, mix until the sugar dissolves and the liquid reduces to a quarter cup. Mix in Tokay and move on a bowl; cover. Refrigerate.

- Using a small and wet knife, run it around the edges of the cake and flip onto baking sheet. Serve cakes with a drizzle of syrup.

## 139. Walnut Crepes With Raspberries And Dried Figs

*"(CREPES DE NOIX AUX FRAMBOISE ET FIGUES)*
*Crepes are often served merely in Provence, together with jam, sugar, or liqueur. They get a little more dressed in this recipe."*
*Serving: Serves 6*

## Ingredients

- 1/2 vanilla bean, split lengthwise
- 1 1/2 cups chopped dried Calimyrna figs
- 1 12-oz. package frozen sweetened raspberries (not packed in syrup), thawed, juice reserved
- 1 cup Muscat wine
- 1 cup water
- 1/4 cup (packed) dark brown sugar
- 2 tbsps. honey
- 2 tsps. orange peel
- 1 cup (or more) whole milk
- 1 cup all purpose flour
- 3 large eggs
- 1/4 cup chopped walnuts
- 2 tbsps. sugar
- 2 tbsps. (1/4 stick) unsalted butter, melted
- 1 tsp. grated orange peel
- 1/4 tsp. salt
- Additional melted butter
- Additional sugar
- 1 8-oz. container crème fraîche*
- 2 tbsps. honey
- *Available at some supermarkets. If unavailable, heat 1 cup whipping cream to lukewarm (85°F.). Remove from heat; mix in 2 tbsps. buttermilk. Cover; let stand in warm draft-free area until slightly thickened, 24 to 48 hours, depending on temperature of room. Chill until ready to use.

## Direction

- For the filling, scrape the seeds from the vanilla bean and put it into the heavy medium saucepan. Add the bean together with the raspberries with juices, figs, and other remaining ingredients. Let the mixture simmer, stirring constantly until the sugar dissolves completely. Simmer over medium heat for 30 more minutes until the figs are tender. Let the mixture cool. (Take note that this can be prepared 3 days ahead. Just keep it covered and chilled.)
- For the crepes, mix a cup of milk and the next seven ingredients in a blender. Process the mixture until smooth, scraping the sides of the blender down occasionally. Cover the blender and chill the crepe batter for 2 hours. Re-blend the batter for 15 seconds. If you want to have a consistency of heavy cream, thin the batter with more milk, adding it 1 tbsp. at a time.
- Heat the nonstick skillet (having a 7-inches diameter bottom) over medium-high heat. Brush the skillet with additional melted butter. Pour scant 1/4 cup crepe batter into the skillet, tilting skillet quickly to coat bottom. Pour scant 1/4 cup crepe batter into the skillet, tilting it quickly to coat bottom. Cook for 35 seconds, loosening the sides of crepe using the spatula until the bottom is golden and the top looks dry. Flip the crepe over. Cook for 20 more seconds until brown spots will form at the bottom. Transfer the crepe onto the plate. Do the same with the remaining batter and stack them on the plate.
- Brush the 13x9x2-inches glass baking dish with extra butter melted. Spoon generous 2 tbsp. of the filling in the middle of the spotted side of the crepe. Within 1 inch of edge, spread filling on the crepe. Fold the crepe in half, and then fold it again in half until it forms a wedge shape. Place the filled crepe into the prepared dish. Do the same with the remaining crepes and filling. Make sure to overlap crepes into the dish slightly. Brush the crepes with melted butter lightly. Lightly sprinkle crepes with sugar. Use a foil to cover the dish. In a small

bowl, mix honey and crème fraiche until well blended. (Take note that the crepes and honey crème fraiche can be prepared a day ahead. Just cover them separately and keep them chilled.)

- Set the oven to 350°F for preheating. Bake the crepes for 20 minutes, covered until heated through. Arrange 2 crepes onto each of the 6 plates. Before serving, top the crepes with a dollop of honey crème fraiche.

## Nutrition Information

- Calories: 509
- Total Carbohydrate: 64 g
- Cholesterol: 137 mg
- Total Fat: 23 g
- Fiber: 6 g
- Protein: 9 g
- Sodium: 177 mg
- Saturated Fat: 11 g

## 140. Walnut Risotto With Roasted Asparagus

*"Rich and flavorful risotto on oven-roasted asparagus."*
*Serving: Serves 4*

## Ingredients

- 4 1/2 to 5 cups canned low-salt chicken broth
- 3 tsps. olive oil (preferably extra virgin)
- 1/3 cup chopped onion
- 1-1/4 cups arborio rice or medium-grain white rice
- 1/2 cup dry white wine
- 1 lb. asparagus, tough ends trimmed
- 1 large garlic clove, thinly sliced
- 1/4 cup finely chopped toasted walnuts
- 2 tbsps. freshly grated Parmesan cheese

## Direction

- Preheat the oven to 450 degrees F. Simmer broth in a medium pot; cover and take off heat. On medium-high heat, heat 1 1/2 tsp

olive oil in a heavy medium pot. Sauté onion for 4mins until light golden; put in rice and mix for a minute. Pour in wine and mix for 2mins until it evaporates. Pour in half cup hot broth; cook and stir frequently until the rice absorbs the liquid. Keep on adding half cup of broth at a time until the rice is creamy and tender. Mix regularly to let the rice absorb broth then add more, 25mins.

- In a shallow baking dish, arrange garlic and asparagus. Pour in leftover 1 1/2 tsp oil; season with pepper and salt. Mix the asparagus and garlic to coat. Bake for 16mins until tender, flip from time to time.
- Stir grated Parmesan and walnuts into the risotto; sprinkle pepper and salt. Place roasted asparagus in the middle of four plates then add risotto on top.

## 141. Warm Beaujolais Kir

*Serving: Makes about 4 cups, serving 4 to 6*

## Ingredients

- A bottle of Beaujolais
- 3/4 cup crème de cassis, or to taste
- Two 3-inch strips of lemon or orange zest removed with a vegetable peeler plus, if desired, lemon or orange slices for garnish

## Direction

- Combine the crème de cassis, Beaujolais and the zest in a pot; stir well. Cover and simmer for five minutes. Remove the zest and serve mixture in wineglasses, garnished with a slice of orange or lemon, or as desired.

## 142. White Sangria

*""This amazing summer party punch comprises ginger ale, cognac, peach schnapps, orange slices, mango and white wine. Awesome stuff!""*
*Serving: 32 | Prep: 30m | Ready in: 1h30m*

### Ingredients

- 1/2 cup peach schnapps
- 1/2 cup cognac
- 1/4 cup white sugar
- 4 oranges, sliced into rounds
- 2 mangos, peeled and sliced
- 4 (750 milliliter) bottles dry white wine, chilled
- 1 liter ginger ale, chilled

### Direction

- Combine sliced mangos, sliced oranges, sugar, cognac and peach schnapps in a pitcher and let it chill for 1 hour. Dispense the fruit mixture into a big punch bowl before stirring in the ginger ale and white wine.

## 143. White Zinfandel Sangria

*"Feel free to experiment with different fresh fruits that are available to you – strawberries, apples, pineapples and mangoes to name a few. Make sure there is a minimum of one citrusy fruit to add some zing to the drink. This sangria is perfect for alfresco luncheons or picnics and it goes really well with savoury foods like paella."*
*Serving: Serves 6*

### Ingredients

- 1 750-ml bottle of chilled White Zinfandel
- 1/2 cup peach schnapps
- 2 tbsps. Cointreau or other orange liqueur
- 2 tbsps. sugar
- 2 cinnamon sticks, broken in half
- 1 lemon, sliced
- 1 orange, sliced
- 1 peach, sliced into wedges

---

- 1 10-oz. bottle of chilled club soda
- Ice cubes

### Direction

- In a tall pitcher, combine the first 8 ingredients. For at least 30 minutes, keep it refrigerated to let the flavors blend together before adding club soda. To serve, insert ice cubes into 6 wineglasses before pouring the sangria over it.

### Nutrition Information

- Calories: 174
- Total Carbohydrate: 17 g
- Total Fat: 0 g
- Fiber: 2 g
- Protein: 1 g
- Sodium: 11 mg
- Saturated Fat: 0 g

## 144. Wild Mushroom And Roasted Garlic Sandwich

*"Want to taste the true flavor of mushroom? Try this mushroom recipe!"*
*Serving: 6 servings*

### Ingredients

- About 1/4 cup extra virgin olive oil
- 2 tbsps. unsalted butter
- 1 lb. mixed wild and domestic mushrooms, such as shiitakes (stems removed), creminis, portobellos, oyster mushrooms, and chanterelles, cleaned and cut into 1-inch pieces.
- Kosher salt
- freshly ground black pepper
- 2 garlic cloves, finely chopped
- 1 shallot, finely chopped
- 1 tsp. chopped fresh thyme
- 1/4 cup dry white wine
- 2 tbsps. chopped fresh parsley

- 12 slices of country-style bread, about 3 inches long and ⅓ inch thick
- 4 whole heads of roasted garlic, cloves squeezed to remove the softened garlic

## Direction

- On medium-high heat, cook 2 tbsps. butter with 3-4 tbsps. olive oil into the big sauté pan until butter is so hot. Toss in your meatiest mushrooms (portobellos or creminis). Cook all sides until mushroom turn lightly brown and start to run out juices for about 5 minutes. Put the remaining mushrooms. Sprinkle salt and pepper; taste. On medium heat, cook continuously the mushrooms, mixing every few minutes, for about another 5 minutes.
- Toss in the shallot, thyme, and freshly sliced garlic. Sauté for about 2 minutes until fragrant. Pour white wine, cook continuously until mushrooms tenderized and most of the wine and juices of mushroom evaporates, for about 10 minutes more. Sprinkle pepper and salt to season. Put in parsley. Keep mushroom warm until use.
- Assembling sandwiches: Toast bread by grilling or broiling on each side until it turns golden brown in color. Spread roasted garlic generously on each piece. Place 6 bread slices on top with the mushrooms. Add the rest of bread slices for covering with the garlic side down.

## 145. Wild Mushroom Soup With Sherry

*"Craving for mushroom soup? Well, here it is! Creamy and tasty mushroom soup with a colonial style."*
*Serving: Makes 8 to 10 servings*

## Ingredients

- 8 tbsps. (1 stick) butter, room temperature
- 2 cups sliced celery
- 1 cup sliced shallots
- 3/4 cup chopped onion

- 3 garlic cloves, minced
- 3 cups sliced stemmed fresh shiitake mushrooms (about 6 oz.)
- 3 cups sliced crimini mushrooms (about 6 oz.)
- 3 cups sliced oyster mushrooms (about 4 1/2 oz.)
- 1/2 cup dry white wine
- 1/2 cup dry Sherry
- 1/4 cup all purpose flour
- 8 cups chicken stock or canned low-salt chicken broth
- 1/2 cup whipping cream

## Direction

- On medium-high heat, add 6 tbsps. of butter in a big pot to melt. Toss in onion, celery, garlic, and shallots; stir-fry until onion turns opaque for about 8 minutes. Toss in all of the mushrooms; stir-fry until starts to soften for about 4 minutes. Pour in Sherry and white wine, allow boiling until the liquid turns to glaze for about 6 minutes.
- In a small sized bowl, combine the 1/4 cup of flour and the rest of 2 tbsps. butter until mixture turns to smooth paste. Add the flour paste into the mushroom mixture in the pot, mixing until dissolved and the vegetables are coated. Slowly stir in the stock. Allow boiling while frequently stirring. Lower heat to medium-low; simmer until mushroom tenderized, mixing often for about 10 minutes. Add in cream; stir. Sprinkle pepper and salt over to season.
- Using a processor or blender, work in batches to mash the soup until smooth. Transfer soup into the pot. (Soup can be done 1 day ahead. Keep in the refrigerator with cover. To use: On medium-low heat, reheat stock. Serve.) Scoop soup using a ladle into the bowls. Serve.

## Nutrition Information

- Calories: 298
- Total Carbohydrate: 22 g
- Cholesterol: 54 mg
- Total Fat: 19 g
- Fiber: 2 g

- Protein: 9 g
- Sodium: 433 mg
- Saturated Fat: 11 g

## 146. Wine-braised Brisket With Butternut Squash

*"The Jews really love their brisket and even the mention of it brings up endless stories of the past. As usual, the brisket needs to be braised for several hours. However, white wine is used in place of the typical red and the potatoes are replaced with butternut squash. The alterations make for a less heavy meal, so that it's better fitted as holiday meals for the warmer months. If you prefer making this a more wintry brisket, you can swap the squash for turnips and/or potatoes and insert the veggies an hour ahead of the stated time."*

*Serving: Serves 6–8*

## Ingredients

- 1 1/2 cups canned diced tomatoes
- 4 cups beef, chicken, or vegetable broth, store-bought or homemade
- 1 (750-mL) bottle white wine (Pinot Grigio, Sauvignon Blanc, etc.)
- 1 tbsp. kosher salt
- 1 tsp. freshly ground black pepper
- 1 tbsp. vegetable oil
- 2 1/2 lbs. second cut brisket (also called deckle)
- 1 large onion, sliced
- Handful of fresh thyme sprigs
- 1 large butternut squash, peeled, seeded, and chopped into large chunks
- Chopped fresh herbs, for serving

## Direction

- Preheat the oven to 300°F.
- Combine salt, pepper, wine, broth and tomatoes in a large bowl.
- Heat oil in a large enamelled Dutch oven with a tight-fitting lid over medium heat. In a pan, sear the meat for 2 to 3 minutes per side or until it is evenly browned.

- Remove the meat and set it aside. Line onion slices on the bottom of the Dutch oven and set the brisket on top of it before pouring the tomato mixture over the meat. Make sure that the meat is thoroughly covered by the mixture. In the case you are using a larger pot and the liquid does not quite cover the meat and vegetables, pour more water in until it does. Throw thyme sprigs.
- Bake in the oven for 3 -1/2 hours, covered. For every hour that passes by, make a quick check to ensure that the liquid is still covering the meat. If it appears that the meat isn't covered at any point, add hot water into the Dutch oven until the meat is covered again. After 3-1/2 hours, insert the butternut squash and push until it is entirely submerged in the liquid. Continue cooking for another hour before moving the pot out of the oven. Before slicing, let it sit for a minimum of 45 minutes.
- The brisket can be kept until the next day and it actually tastes even better that way, after being reheated in the oven. Transfer about 3 cups of liquid from the Dutch oven into a small saucepot to serve. Over medium-low heat, cook until it reduce into a sauce. Place the squash and brisket on a platter then ladle sauce over it. Garnish with some fresh herbs.

## Nutrition Information

- Calories: 721
- Total Carbohydrate: 22 g
- Cholesterol: 178 mg
- Total Fat: 45 g
- Fiber: 4 g
- Protein: 36 g
- Sodium: 1155 mg
- Saturated Fat: 17 g

## 147. Wine-braised Leg Of Lamb With Garlic

*"Enjoy this meal properly with a full-bodied Zinfandel. There are a few things that make this recipe unique, two alterations specifically. For one, the red wine is replaced by a white. For another, a big complete leg is used instead of the typical small shanks."*
*Serving: Makes 6 servings*

### Ingredients

- 1 5 3/4-lb. bone-in leg of lamb, well trimmed
- 4 large garlic cloves, minced, divided
- 3 large heads of garlic, cut horizontally in half
- 1 bunch fresh thyme (about 1 oz.)
- 1 750-ml bottle dry white wine (such as Chardonnay)
- 2 tbsps. (1/4 stick) butter

### Direction

- Preheat the oven to 475°F. In a big roasting pan, set the lamb down and use 1/2 of minced garlic to massage all over it. Scatter some pepper and salt.
- Prepare halved heads of garlic around lamb and cut side up. All over and around the lamb, sprinkle a bunch of thyme. For 20 minutes, roast the lamb. Lower the temperature of the oven to 350°F. Pour wine into a big saucepan and boil for 5 minutes. Dispense the wine on areas surrounding the lamb and cover it up. For another 2 hours and 45 minutes, continue cooking and roasting until the lamb becomes extremely tender. (Cook one day in advance if preferred. Just remember to let it cool down without any cover on for an hour before refrigerating it with a cover on. Before proceeding, heat it up for half an hour with a cover on in 350°F oven). Move the knobs of garlic and lamb onto a platter and use foil to tent. From the pan of juices, remove the garlic skins and thyme sprigs with a slotted spoon. Over moderately high, put the roasting pan on the stovetop. Boil the juices before inserting the rest of the minced garlic as well as the butter. For around 12 minutes, let the juices boil until it turns a little thick. Scatter pepper and salt onto the jus to season it. Cut the lamb up and put the jus over it with a spoon.

### Nutrition Information

- Calories: 901
- Total Carbohydrate: 16 g
- Cholesterol: 241 mg
- Total Fat: 53 g
- Fiber: 1 g
- Protein: 65 g
- Sodium: 206 mg
- Saturated Fat: 24 g

## 148. Wine-braised Pork Loin

*"Delicious pork accompanied by a flavourful sauce, what a great meal! It requires quite a bit of prep work, but the actual cooking process is pretty simple."*
*Serving: Serves 6*

### Ingredients

- 2 tsps. salt
- 1/2 tsp. ground pepper
- 1 bay leaf, crumbled
- 1 garlic clove, minced
- Pinch of ground allspice
- 1 2-lb. boned center-cut pork loin roast, rolled, tied
- 3 tbsps. olive oil
- 2 onions, chopped
- 4 garlic cloves, chopped
- 2 red bell peppers, cut lengthwise into strips, halved crosswise
- 1 cup dry white wine
- 1 cup canned crushed tomatoes with added puree
- 1 cup canned beef broth
- 2 bay leaves
- 1 tbsp. dried marjoram, crumbled

## Direction

- In a small bowl, mix the first 5 ingredients together. Pat the pork dry before rubbing salt mixture all over it. Cover it up and let it chill for 6 hours or overnight.
- Preheat the oven to 350°F. Wipe the pork until dry. In a sturdy Dutch oven or casserole, heat 2 tbsps. of oil over high heat then add the pork. Cook for 10 minutes until it's browned on all sides. Move it to a plate and lower the heat down to a medium. Insert the remaining 1-tbsp. of oil into the Dutch oven, followed by the onions. Sauté for around 10 minutes until they turn very tender then add the peppers and garlic. Sauté for another 5 minutes until the peppers start to soften then add the marjoram, bay leaves, tomatoes, wine and broth. Add the pork with its fat side up, along with the drippings on the plate. Bring it to a boil and cover it up. Bake for 45 minutes until tender. Move the pork to a platter and leave it standing for 15 minutes. Boil the sauce until it reduces to 4 cups if needed and season with pepper and salt. (This can be prepped one day in advance, just make sure it is covered up and chilled. Pour half the sauce into a baking dish, put the pork slices on top then pour the remaining sauce over the meat. Warm it up again in a covered dish at 350°F in the oven for 30 minutes until thoroughly heated.) Serve the pork together with sauce.

## Nutrition Information

- Calories: 364
- Total Carbohydrate: 11 g
- Cholesterol: 74 mg
- Total Fat: 22 g
- Fiber: 3 g
- Protein: 26 g
- Sodium: 808 mg
- Saturated Fat: 6 g

## 149. Wine-braised Red Cabbage

*"A hearty and yummy meal starring potatoes, cabbage and apple, cooked in wine."*
*Serving: Makes 4 servings*

## Ingredients

- 2 tbsps. (1/4 stick) butter
- 2 1/2 cups thinly sliced red cabbage
- 1/2 cup chopped peeled Granny Smith apple
- 1/4 cup chopped red onion
- 1 bacon slice, chopped
- 1/4 cup dry red wine
- 2 tbsps. red wine vinegar
- 1/2 cup finely grated peeled russet potato
- 1 tbsp. honey

## Direction

- In a big, sturdy skillet, melt the butter over medium heat then add the bacon, onion, apple and cabbage. Sauté for about 6 minutes until cabbage becomes crisp-tender then add the vinegar and wine. Cover it up and cook for about 10 minutes until liquid has evaporated and the cabbage has turned tender. Insert the honey and potato then cover it up. Cook for about 3 minutes until the potato turns tender. Use salt and pepper to season the cabbage mixture to desired taste.

## Nutrition Information

- Calories: 149
- Total Carbohydrate: 15 g
- Cholesterol: 20 mg
- Total Fat: 9 g
- Fiber: 2 g
- Protein: 2 g
- Sodium: 65 mg
- Saturated Fat: 5 g

## 150. Wuxi Spareribs

*"These spare ribs are one of Little Shanghai's signature dishes and rightly so, as it's very delicious."*
*Serving: Makes 4 servings(as part of a Chinese meal)*

## Ingredients

- 1 scallion, trimmed, plus 1 tbsp. chopped scallion
- 1 lb. pork spareribs, cut crosswise into 2-inch pieces by butcher
- 1/3 cup Chinese rice wine (preferably Shaoxing) or medium-dry Sherry
- 1 tbsp. regular soy sauce (sometimes labeled "thin")
- 1 tbsp. dark soy sauce (sometimes labeled "superior")
- 3 cups plus 1 tbsp. water
- 1 (1/2-inch) piece fresh ginger, peeled and cut crosswise into 1/8-inch-thick slices
- 1 1/2 tsps. star anise pieces (not whole)
- 1 (3-inch) cinnamon stick
- 1 1/2 tbsps. coarsely crushed yellow rock sugar (sometimes labeled "yellow rock candy")
- 1 tsp. coarsely ground black pepper
- 1 tsp. cornstarch
- 1 tsp. Asian sesame oil
- 1 tbsp. chopped fresh cilantro

## Direction

- In a pot (4 quart) of boiling water, blanch a whole scallion for 1 minute or until softened before moving scallion to a work surface and return pot of water to boil. Add the ribs to boiling water then draining it with a colander at once. Move the ribs into a 2-1/2 to 3-quart wide, heavy pot. Tie the blanched scallion carefully into a knot and place into the pot with ribs.
- Add pepper, sugar, cinnamon, anise, ginger, soy sauces, wine and 3 cups of water. Cover and let it simmer for about 1 hour until meat is just tender. Remove the lid. Over medium-high heat, boil and stir from time to time for 20 more minutes. It is ready when the sauce reduces by 3/4 and the meat becomes

extremely tender. In a cup, whisk the remaining tbsp. of water and corn-starch together. Lower the heat down to medium and mix the corn-starch mixture to the ribs. Cook for around 1 minute until the sauce thickens, stir. Move it away from the heat and stir in the sesame oil. Before serving, sprinkle with cilantro and chopped scallion.

## Nutrition Information

- Calories: 373
- Total Carbohydrate: 9 g
- Cholesterol: 91 mg
- Total Fat: 28 g
- Fiber: 1 g
- Protein: 19 g
- Sodium: 541 mg
- Saturated Fat: 9 g

# Index

# Conclusion

Thank you again for downloading this book!

I hope you enjoyed reading about my book!

If you enjoyed this book, please take the time to share your thoughts and post a review on Amazon. It'd be greatly appreciated!

Write me an honest review about the book – I truly value your opinion and thoughts and I will incorporate them into my next book, which is already underway.

Thank you!

If you have any questions, **feel free to contact at:** _msingredient@mrandmscooking.com_

Ms. Ingredient

www.MrandMsCooking.com

Printed in Great Britain
by Amazon